"Through this fetching memoir, Berghoef shows us that religion can be wonderful but is sometimes a terrible trap. But that's just a warm up for the actual mission of this wonderful book. Great writing aside—and it is great writing—this is a how-to on rediscovering faith by escaping our frightened rigidity."

—FRANK SCHAEFFER, AUTHOR OF *CRAZY FOR GOD*

"Christine is a great storyteller! From growing up in a warm but incredibly conservative church in West Michigan to being recruited to serve Republican powerbrokers as a member of the secretive family in Washington, Christine's description of her faith journey never bores. What she finally reveals is that to grow up in the faith you may have to set aside simple structures and ancient doctrines for a new and transforming encounter with the Word."

—JOHN SUK, AUTHOR OF *NOT SURE*

Cracking the Pot

Cracking the Pot

Releasing God from the Theologies that Bind Him

Christine Berghoef

RESOURCE *Publications* · Eugene, Oregon

Resource Publications
An Imprint of Wipf and Stock Publishers
199 W. 8th Ave., Suite 3
Eugene, OR 97401
www.wipfandstock.com

ISBN 13: 978-1-61097-653-4

Manufactured in the U.S.A.

For the theological doubters
who dared to speak,

and all those who dare not.

The matter is quite simple.
The Bible is very easy to understand.
But we Christians are a bunch of scheming swindlers.
We pretend to be unable to understand it because we know very well
that the minute we understand, we are obliged to act accordingly.

Take any words in the New Testament and forget everything
except pledging yourself to act accordingly.
My God, you will say,
if I do that my whole life will be ruined.
How would I ever get on in the world?

Herein lies the real place of Christian scholarship.
Christian scholarship is the Church's prodigious invention to
defend itself against the Bible, to ensure that we can continue to be
good Christians without the Bible coming too close.

Oh priceless scholarship, what would we do without you?
Dreadful it is to fall into the hands of the living God.
Yes, it is even dreadful to be alone
with the New Testament.

—SØREN KIERKEGAARD

Contents

Acknowledgments

I'M EVER GRATEFUL FOR those who have and who continue to support and cheer me on as I clumsily jump around in the ring facing my doubts, questions, and quandaries in this wrestling match that seems unending.

Thanks to my friends at Cuppa Joe and Xylo, for providing me space to write, and for keeping the coffee flowing.

Thanks to those of you who gave my first draft a read through, demonstrating generous hospitality to my vulnerabilities.

I'm so grateful to the Thursday morning "church ladies." You provided ears for my occasional theological and political ramblings and expressed great love and encouragement to me throughout my writing.

Thanks to David Rylaarsdam and John Suk, for encouragement and feedback on various bits of church history.

Special thanks to Chris Lubbers and Doug Koopman, for meticulously sweeping over the manuscript, providing thoughtful and creative "big picture" insights, as well as helping me smooth out the fine wrinkles. You helped me find the words to traverse the rocks I could not find my way around. Your friendship, understanding, encouragement, criticisms, and dialogue with me throughout the process have meant more to me than you'll ever know.

Thanks to my editor and dear friend, Gaynor Lubojasky, for taming the atrocious grammatical beast I sent you and for cleaning up my, excessive, use, of, commas. You have been such a steady stream of encouragement all along the way.

Tremendous gratitude to my parents for always loving me.

And deepest thanks to my family, who made sacrifices when I was off writing somewhere. To my sweet peanuts—Henry, Winston, Charles, and Josephine for sometimes enduring quickly thrown-together, unbalanced meals, and for returning remarkable patience to me when I was stressed out and impatient with you.

Acknowledgments

Thanks to my husband, Bryan, for so much love, patience, dish-washing, potty training, and home schooling in my absence. For giving me space to write and for reading (and editing!) multiple versions of the manuscript with an eye to letting the language flow. And above all, thank you for hanging on to me when the world seemed to fall out from beneath my feet.

Author's Note

THIS BOOK IS BASED on my personal recollections and research. In so far as the book describes my inner spiritual journey and the conclusions I came to, it is one hundred percent true. Some names and descriptions of people in the book have been changed to protect their privacy.

I took creative license in portions of the book by making a composite of multiple real-life conversations, and sometimes people. Many events are, no doubt, recalled imperfectly, but their description reflects the way I remember them and the ongoing impact they have on my life.

Introduction

ON THE CALENDAR OF my life, the early days mark the beginning of my simple path of faith, before the adult stuff kicked in, before innocence lost out to the complexities of an intricate and complicated world, before all the basic black and white truths became smeared. I was raised in a good family, experienced a happy childhood, and was indoctrinated into a specific religious background.

As I grew and began stretching my arms into the sleeves of adulthood, contradicting emotions pulled me in two directions. I wanted things to remain forever the same in my untainted world and, at the same time, I grew desperate to break away and experience the world that I gradually realized existed outside of the forty acres I grew up on.

In the discovery of this larger world, my childhood perceptions collided with a tidal wave of contrasting ideas, religions, philosophies, cultures, and worldviews. I became shocked to discover that most people had never even heard of the denomination in which I was raised, the Christian Reformed Church (CRC). I suddenly faced many questions that I simply could not answer, or found that I simply could no longer accept answers of old. Despite my upbringing being grounded in a high level of certainty, I found myself unprepared in the face of everyone else's contrasting certainties.

This book largely relates my personal story of the people, circumstances, philosophies, and cultural encounters that impacted, molded, and sometimes shattered my simple faith. This process brought to the surface many questions—questions for which my tidy, outlined answers ultimately proved insufficient.

I invite you to experience my journey thus far. If you grew up in a tradition similar to mine, you may well resonate with parts of it—I hope you're able to laugh a little, cry a little, and also appreciate the gift you've been given. If you're easily offended by hyperbole or scant amounts of sarcasm, then I suggest you not turn even one more page. You may even be able to secure a refund for this book if you go no further and return it today. I aim occasional jabs at my own subjective view of my personal experiences, always with the intention of pointing toward a larger truth.

In the first chapter, I lay out the foundation upon which my faith and all my perspectives about life were built. I was like a seed planted in a pot, a pot filled with the goodness, love, and religion of my childhood. My parents, family, church friends, and community, in varying proportions, added soil comprised of a specific set of values and beliefs. Under their careful attention, the seed was designed to grow into a plant of the same species as all the other plants in the garden.

Subsequent chapters relate my sometimes immature and irreverent perspective during my adolescent years. I dared myself to be vulnerable with you in sharing some of my most intimate thoughts and honest reflections of that time in my life to give you a picture of some of the attitudes that my idyllic subculture unintentionally fostered.

From there, the book jumps to life beyond college graduation, when I was suddenly thrust into the world and more fully exposed to other realities. This was the time when big questions began surfacing and swirling in my head, staking claims on the territory of my sleep. Through the pages, my childhood voice slowly shifts and becomes its own adult voice.

I walked, and sometimes crawled, through an intense period of questioning, going through encounters and experiences that eventually led me to a place of doubting everything about God and my faith. With doubt came loss of identity, followed by isolation and despair. But out of the tilled soils of despair, a new faith slowly began to sprout. Examining my certainties led me to many uncertainties, and then finally full circle to a place of a basic, simplistic faith once again. Through this journey, I discovered a new place where my faith can grow, even in the midst of life's swarming complexities.

While the book ends where I presently am in my faith walk, my journey is by no means over. I continue to seek truth, to ask questions, to experience doubt, to find rest in the uncertainties, to examine my life by the measure of the one I seek to follow. Though this has often resulted in rejecting one certainty or another from my childhood subculture, it has been part of my path in seeking authenticity in my faith. I have no doubt that this quest for such a faith is, ironically, a result of the deep authenticity of the two beautiful people who came together in love, nurtured me all those years, and gently nudged me out into the world.

I invite you to join me in asking questions. I invite you to discuss these questions and dialogue within yourself and in community with others. I hope you will permit yourself an honest slice of time to question your certainties and reexamine your life in light of these questions. I've found it to be a good and healthy process, and it's my prayer that it becomes that for you as well.

Christine Berghoef

CHAPTER 1

The Planting

A Look Back

FOR THE MOST PART, my childhood was an idyllic one. Perhaps not exactly the stuff of fairy tales, but certainly I had my castles, my kingdoms, and my many adventures with their happily-ever-after endings.

Our forty acres sat on the southern outskirts of Holland, Michigan, between the charming Norman Rockwellesque villages of Graafschap and the farm-dotted East Saugatuck. On our farm, we tended some beef cattle, a herd of Angora goats, a couple milk cows, a generous vegetable garden, a variety of fruit trees, and a flock of chickens on the loose. Past the fields, woods arose with trails blazed through, along with a creek that moseyed along the forest floor—twisting with the curves of the earth—between a variety of hardwoods, under bridges, and finally pooling itself up against a dam.

I lived among those trees, calling them by name, possessing a deep knowing of them and the various mosses softening the tips of their callous feet. We were kindred spirits, developing and maturing together under all the weather of the world. Fields of alfalfa whispered in the breeze near large, fenced-in pastures where the goats and cattle grazed. My grandparents lived in a small house on the far corner of our farm, and my cousins lived on the forty acres across the street.

If the world had anything more to offer, I was oblivious to it.

My young, ambitious parents had two paramount priorities. First, a private Christian education for the kids, and second, having Mom home with us during those critical early years. If you have any idea as to the cost of a private education for four children, then you will understand the difficulty in achieving both of these measures simultaneously. Through lots of hard work and sacrifice, they set the goal and somehow achieved it.

We lived a fairly simple life of second-hand and homemade clothes in our early years. We had only a few toys, but I never felt shorted as the whole forty-acre world was my playground, full of organic, endless, self-made entertainment.

We attempted to be as self-sustaining as possible. Between a pasture of grazing cattle and the hunting season—which inevitably brought in a few deer—meat remained plentiful. No piece of animal went wasted. The family would form an assembly line as we cut, wrapped and labeled the steaks, roasts, and soup bones for year-round grazing from the freezer. The hides were made into rugs or sold. During the winter months, we strung up thinly sliced smoked cuts of beef and venison jerky over the wood-burning stove to dry. I frequently gave in to the temptation of prematurely tearing off small corners of the hanging pieces as the smoky scent rendered me incapable of resisting. Salted large chunks of meat would hang in the smokehouse several weeks at a time, ultimately becoming dried beef and venison, always delicious carved up and sandwiched with cheese between slices of Mom's homemade bread.

Sliced up cow tongue sandwiches made an occasional, delightful treat while we fought over the largest piece of heart. Sautéed liver and onions, detested by us kids, kept us chained to the table, as we weren't allowed to leave until we had licked our plates clean. We managed to find ways to make the liver tolerable—such as dousing it with ketchup and plugging our noses while we chewed—in order to dumb down the sense of the taste buds. Thankfully, Dad never required us to eat boiled kidneys; the smell literally sent me running from the house retching in the shrubbery. But he ate them. Nothing wasted. If at my cousin's house, across the street and slightly downwind, I would smell the horrible putrid scent of boiled kidneys wafting from the open windows of my house, I would invite myself to dine with my cousins. Nothing in the whole world was worse to me than having to endure that stink.

Brandishing his 12-gauge shotgun, Dad also hunted rabbits. I loved trailing along with him. We kids had the noble task of mounting the brush piles and jumping, until the unsuspecting rabbits would dart out from under the copious mounds of tangled branches. Little tasted as good as baked, barbecued rabbit. We ingested the tender muscle of bunny and sucked the bones dry. For me, a bonus treasure would appear in the form of a silky-soft bunny tail to pinch between my fingers, tenderly brush over my cheeks, and nestle in my fist while I sucked my thumb in bed at night. You might think I would have desired one of the rabbit's feet for good luck, but I much preferred the soft tail for sweet dreams.

Sometimes in the summers, my parents sent us kids to the pond with a can of night-crawlers fresh from the earth, a bucket, and our rods and reels. When the bucket filled up with enough bluegill to appease everyone around the dinner table, we headed home to scale, cut, and clean our catch of the day.

Eggs from the chickens and milk from the milk cows also provided nourishment for our family. Unable to resist sentimental urges, Dad occasionally took to making cheese, cottage cheese, yogurt, ice cream, and butter. More fresh cream skimmed from the top of the bucket remained than we could put away, so we kept the dozen barn cats fat on it.

Our patch of earth that produced vegetables always seemed bountiful. As children, our assigned tasks consisted of helping out with the planting, the weeding, the hoeing, and the harvesting. Few other duties seemed both so dreaded and so satisfying as this feeling of being connected to the earth. I loved—still love—the touch and the scent of the dirt turning over in my hands. I savored the sound when the roots of the weeds ripped from their entrenched grip on the ground beneath. Harvesting the vegetables, picking apples, pears, grapes, and berries, we would fill and refill our various buckets until the picking stained and numbed our small fingers.

And then, in the company of her liltingly sweet voice, Mom quietly sang as she worked in the kitchen—bent over the many varieties of fruits and vegetables—canning, pickling, freezing, and drying. I got a kick out of watching the canning jars, with their many goods and variety of colors, increase on the kitchen counters, lined up like little soldiers. After the cooling process finished, announced by the popping sound of the lids as the vacuum within sucked them down with a snap, we carefully transported them to the many shelves in the dark, dank basement. Root vegetables—such as beets, carrots, potatoes, rutabaga, sweet potatoes, and squash—we dug up with flat spades and stored in bushel baskets in the underground storm shelter, a cement bunker buried in the backyard.

The menu didn't consist solely of fruits, vegetables, and meat, though. We had sweets as well. Dad kept a few bees for honey. We counted little else in the world as delicious as a bite of smackingly sweet, dripping honeycomb. Chewing the soft wax as honey oozed from it was like Christmas in my mouth. We also tapped maple trees in the woods, gathering the sap in the spring, and boiling it down to precious gold: syrup, sugar, and candy.

Always grateful for the stretching afternoons of summer, I delighted in all there was to be known during those brilliantly sunny days. We all had our several chores to do year round, but summer brought us together in community for various seasonal responsibilities as well. Baling comes to mind. Much of the family became involved in some way—my parents, siblings, aunt, uncles, cousins, Grandpa and Grandma. The Massey-Ferguson mesmerizingly pulled the baler as it scooped up the cut and dried grasses, rolling it through the hidden premises of mechanical genius and transforming it into a perfectly lovely, rectangular, bundled bale of alfalfa. I could scarcely imagine such inventiveness. Despite these long workdays that left our bodies aching at the end of them, the smell of the process— a sweet combination of grasses, sweat, and earth—hinted of something divine.

The tractor meandered through the fields hitched to the hay wagon. The baler grasped the grasses and performed its job, sending the bales up to the wagon behind. We strategically stacked the bales of hay on the wagon by means of people standing on various levels of bales, with a procession of bales tossed from person to person and level to level. Grandma and Mom would make—and deliver to the field—Country Time Lemonade and sandwiches on thick-cut homemade bread to replenish our gritty, dust-clung, sweaty bodies. For a mid-day break, we often stripped down to our undergarments, revealing our authentic farmer tan lines, and took a refreshing dive in the pond.

When the wagon became full, we backed up to the barn and rode the long elevator up to the rafters, stacking the hay bales, settling them in for the long winter ahead, and sparing them from the elements. Just as we grew and preserved our food for the extensive winter months, so we also grew and preserved sufficient food for the duration of those same months for our goats and cattle.

When the official baling days ended, my brothers, cousins and I spent our days re-stacking the bales, creating winding tunnels and cavernous rooms: hay forts. Between our many castles in the hay and the various levels of hand-hewn pine rafters in the barn, which we climbed over, around, and across, inventive games always ensued. It's a miracle one of us never fell and snapped a neck. My busy, trusting mother remained completely unaware of our all barn antics.

Other summer activities would fill my days as well. We lived only a mile from "the tracks." The gang of us cousins pedaled our banana-seat bikes, sometimes two or three to a bike—one on the handlebars and two on the seat—down to the rails to tape coins on the tracks. Sometimes we waited in the wild shrubbery for the train to pass, and then we would retrieve the smooshed and smeared faces of Lincoln, Jefferson, and sometimes Washington, if we could afford him. On our way back home, we always scavenged the sides of the road for all the ten-cent refund cans we could find.

After turning in our cans for cash, we counted the coins and saved them until some Saturday when we could make the five-mile bike trip to Graafschap Grocery. There, we spent long periods of time drooling over the variety of candy bars and Dutch sweets in stock before making our selections.

I occasionally spent my summer nights sleeping under the deep expansive vault of celestial activity out in the fields, on the crest of a hill. Lying on my back, it was easy to get lost in the multitude of stars and planets circling above. Very much a part of the universe, I became sharply aware of my smallness in it, and even more appreciative of my significance within the whole of it. My thoughts would drift to God and heaven and I wondered where it all could be found, and why in the midst of this absolutely breathtaking vastness, he chose to come down to me, a mere breath in the span of time.

I had my secret quiet spot on the farm: the crest of the hill in a wide-open alfalfa field. Pushing down the grasses, I created a soft bed, and laid down on my back. For hours, I completely disappeared into daydreams or tracked the movement of the clouds, which seemed like living, breathing creatures ever-migrating eastward. Even in the deep of winter, I would lie in this spot as if in the center of a snow globe, curious about the unexpected warmth of snow, watching the white fleetly dusting over me. A sense of being a participating observer in the changing of the seasons grew within me, as the earth slowly circled the sun. I became a first-hand witness to these unfolding changes. With a sensitive awareness, I silently absorbed it all. In my stillness, I experienced the inevitable change in the world around me in the same way I imagined the unmoving trees and grasses that surrounded me must have understood it.

≈ ≈ ≈

Winter inevitably arrived, bearing gifts of frigid temperatures, swirling snowdrifts, and new chores. We had to saw, haul, split, and stack wood for the wood-burning stove, our source of heat. I recall a few nights so cold in my upstairs bedroom, after the fire had faded, that the cup of water on my nightstand froze solid by morning. Yet I, in my several layers of blankets that somehow remained snug, never felt the crisp air until the rooster crowed. Dancing out of bed in the morning, I swiped my clothes and made swift time across the icy wood floors and down the steps to hover over the freshly warmed wood-burning stove. I momentarily draped my clothes over the stove to warm them and then quickly transferred that heat to my body.

Winter brought about other activities as well: ice skating, snowshoeing, sledding, building snow forts, igloos, and cross country skiing. At night I often strapped my feet into my cross-country skis or hide-bound snowshoes and ventured out under the velvet moon. Something about the snow seemed to muffle all sound. Surrounded by the snow, it was easy to lose myself in it. The absolute stillness of the earth brought an absolute stillness to my soul. It was medicinal. It was a treasure, a gift in its precise time.

Late winter and into early spring, the cattle would give birth. I loved being a part of the process. Dad gathered us to the barn, sometimes rousing us from our sleep if it happened at night. My empathy was most likely developed in these moments. It was terribly painful to watch the mother cow in such intense struggle and physical grief, and yet at the same time, I was unable to peel myself away. I could feel myself pushing with her, breathing heavy with her, wanting to bellow out with her. And when finally—after so much agony—the wet calf emerged (sometimes with a little help from Dad), the warm, sickly, sweet smell of fresh birth permeated the barn. My eyes filled. For me, this was the scent of alleviation, relief that her malaise had ended, that her calf had finally come to suckle at her swollen nipples. The whole process gifted me with an astute awareness that pain is inextricably linked to life. (No need to mention that it also served as a raw, unrefined, first-hand, tactile education as to what lay in store for me someday.)

My father, a tenderhearted man, balanced a nearly perfect combination of both sensitivity and firmness—a loving disciplinarian. In addition to running our small farm, he taught history at a local public school. Flawlessly honest, he had the respect of all who knew him and everyone who did business with him. He possessed (and still possesses) a caliber of integrity rarely seen in today's world.

In my fifth grade year, Dad sold the goats and the cattle and decided to give the business of raising gladiolas a try. He largely tended to the flower farm, named Ottawa Glad Growers, in the summers between his school terms. Dad tilled up the pastures, and we planted rows and rows of gladiola bulbs. When I turned twelve years old, I started spending my summers on my hands and knees, pulling acres of weeds up and down the rows that seemed never to end. When the flowers began to bloom, we cut and bundled them. This, for two dollars an hour. Lest you think it an unfair wage, a full-sized candy bar cost a mere 15 cents in those days. I was quite thrilled and proud to receive and deposit my check at the end of the week, to slowly build up my very own savings account.

Then, after 37 years of teaching, Dad retired. The flower business really took off. He started to grow more and more varieties of flowers, delivering them to florists and selling them at markets. It quickly became a year-round workload, and he grew more passionate about this work, always browsing through seed catalogues like a kid in a candy store, eager to try new things. As the business continued to grow, he hired a good handful of people, at fairly generous wages. The florists commented how privileged they were to do business with such a kind and honest man.

In the days before kids, Mom was a nurse, but she left work to stay home with us when my three brothers and I arrived one by one. It was important to her to nurture us with the sort of love only a mother can truly provide. She was a woman of grace, composed of a rare and gentle, selfless substance. She embodied the fruit of the Spirit—love, joy, peace, patience, kindness goodness, gentleness, faithfulness, and self-control. I envisioned her face when I read the Beatitudes.

She always put others first. She never ever complained when life would hand her the short stick but, instead, always responded with peace and joy. She possessed a quiet spirit, yet a strength that refused to buy into the latest advertised trends. People were always drawn to her. Frequently asked what it's like to have such a remarkable woman for a mom, I was often reminded of the rare and beautiful gift that my mother was (and is).

When we children were all of school age, Mom returned to nursing full time. She worked third shift so she could be home every day to greet us at the door when bus five dropped us off after school. I've always thought that if I could become even half the woman and mother she is, I would be a great one.

Grandpa and Grandma Lubbers, my father's parents, also were a significant part of my life. My after-school routine usually involved quickly taking care of my chores and then sauntering through the fields and forest to Gramp and Grams' house for milk and ginger snaps, followed by a few competitive rounds of either checkers or caroms with Gramps.

He inevitably would have the old checkerboard—cracked, taped and re-taped at the seam—open and ready on his leather-topped footstool. Before the game began, I sat at his feet for a few stories of the "olden days." Gramps grew up on the South Dakota prairie and developed a thick skin over the course of the Great Depression. He held me spellbound with his knack for storytelling. With the game underway, I usually absorbed some political ramblings and theological musings at the same time. In his later years, as age and its forgetfulness began claiming him, I would, more and more, tell his stories back to him.

Grams was a gentle, quiet woman, kind and sweet in every classic grandma sense. Those closest to her knew of a thin streak of independence that ran through her. She, too, had an extremely challenging childhood on the prairies of South Dakota. Scarred knees grew tough from so many years of praying. As a child, I loved sitting beside Grams as she read to me the same few stories over and over and over. In high school, while my friends attended hyped-up school basketball games, I often opted to spend the night sleeping over at Gramp and Grams' house instead. Their cozy house was like a second home to me, and I intuitively knew that they were a special gift that wouldn't be around forever.

Gramp and Grams and the rest of us all attended a middle-sized Christian Reformed Church (CRC)—a church on a hill—hemmed in by a small village where everyone knew everyone, and everyone knew everyone's business. Even this church was like a picture from a child's storybook with its pipe organ and rows of polished wooden pews, tall windows—stained glass at the top—and a bell tower visible from all the surrounding countryside. All the folks who inhabited that countryside could hear its distinctive clanging at the beginning of each church service. Pretty women and little girls in their Sunday dresses, white gloves and delicate little handkerchiefs with crocheted edges, along with handsome men and boys in their suits with hair carefully parted and neatly brushed, filtered in and out of the doors every Sunday.

In and around these forty acres, the simplicity of life marked my pot of faith and ideas about life. A farm-fed, well-groomed, greatly manicured, well-loved, and tended to childhood set me on a faith journey of certainty. My pot, early on, was filled with goodness. I *knew* that my family loved me—I could smell it in my mother's perfume pressed close to me when I was afraid, and I touched it when my father carried my limp body home when I'd fallen asleep in the car late at night. I *knew* my religion—I could feel its crispness in the pressed cotton dresses and smell its goodness like a freshly baked loaf of bread, comforting me to the core. I *knew* my life would certainly proceed in a fashion quite fashioned by these forty acres.

CHAPTER TWO

The Potter's Hands

My chest tightens as I struggle to inhale deeply, my fifteen-year-old self feeling like the claustrophobic, soon-to-be-next victim in one of those senseless horror flicks. The pendulum of life or death swings precariously on this moment. I am about to be called in before the elders of my church to have my faith and theology questioned. I need their approval to be officially approved as a professing member of the Christian Reformed Church. Sitting outside the council room door, I review select portions of the Heidelberg Catechism that I've duly committed to memory, waiting to be called in. Waiting for the information in my head to be dissected, questioned, examined. Waiting.

My big night has finally arrived. I wring my hands together, nervously roll up and release the slack line of my belt, and catch the occasional sweat drop with the back of my shirt sleeve. Certain I will stumble over a word of the Catechism and be denied access to heaven, my breath rolls like a marathon runner in the final stretch.

The clock ticks loudly, fragmenting my thought process, mixing up the answers as I review them over and over in my head. It's reminiscent of when I'm relaxing in my bedroom spinning Amy Grant on my record player, and my little brother comes in and starts jumping, causing the needle to thump around on the record, mixing up phrases, and skipping to the next song halfway through the previous one. As I sit here outside the council room door, my memory also starts skipping: "Question and Answer One: What is your only comfort in life and in death? I am not my own, but I belong in life and in death, body and soul, to my faithful Savior Jesus Christ." *No, wait, that's not it,* I think, reminding myself to focus. "I belong body and soul, in life and in death, to my faithful Savior Jesus

Christ." *That's it,* I nod to myself with satisfaction. With my eternal life on the line, I can't mess this up.

The looming wooden door swings open and, with internal fear and trembling, I enter the room, sitting in the seat motioned for me. Turns out this is at the butt end of a mile-long, pristinely polished wooden table surrounded by pristinely polished, all-knowing, ever intimidating, gray-haired, glasses-hanging-on-the-edge-of-their-noses men staring down at me. Diploma-styled frames line the walls, filled with black-and-white photographs. The stoic faces of all of the previous pastors of the church stare ahead, as if they too are present at this meeting, waiting to judge and devour me. I work hard to maintain my composure and steady my breath, while at the same time exerting reverence and excitement over this big moment in my faith journey.

The whole meeting remains a blur to me, except one thing: I pass. A few weeks later, I stand before the congregation to declare my faith publically, to answer the rehearsed questions with "I do," and with great pride to accept my brand new *Halley's Bible Handbook* in one hand and the golden certificate of Profession of Faith—my ticket to heaven—in the other hand. I can relax a bit now. Our theology claims, "Once saved always saved," so I know for certain that I am "in."

The timing of Profession of Faith is important. There's a critical window of time in which one should do it—not too young because you need to have formally studied the Catechism at some level, which doesn't begin until high school. But if you don't make profession of faith before you graduate from high school, then you might as well forget it because the iniquitous world will grab hold of you and sweep you away into the depths of hell. Like a thick slab of beef on the grill, timing is everything. Keeping it on too little time results in an undercooked, unsafe, and unready steak. But wait too long, and it will burn to a crisp. BURN to a crisp. Parched, burnt meat is never a good thing. I came off the grill a delicious medium rare.

My family and I faithfully and devotedly attend a conservative Christian Reformed Church. Going to morning service is a no-brainer, but one always knows who the *truly devoted* Christians are because they *never* miss the evening service. The evening service is always a smaller crowd but we are there with rare exceptions, so I've grown up knowing that our family is one of the good ones.

So critical is our attendance that if one of us feels sick, my parents use vomit as the litmus test. If we aren't losing our breakfast, we aren't sick enough to justify our absence. Occasionally, the evidence presents itself all over the pew, down the front of my dress, or heaven forbid, on the back of the pinstriped suit in front of me, at which point my dad gives the nod. We are confirmed, in fact, sick. And thank goodness for all the witnesses present in the sanctuary so there will be no whispering and speculative gossiping over our absence.

At church, everyone must sit motionless and soundless in the rock-hard wooden pews. As a young child, I recall desperately wanting to be good, wanting so badly to please the Holy Lord, but try as I did, I was simply unable to focus for so long, and I felt terrible for it. My mind seemed to have a mind of its own.

As a high schooler, time ticks by like molasses during church services. As soon as the service begins, I unknowingly train my mind automatically to go somewhere else. A few options keep me focused on something, anything to pass the hour. The vast stretches between "Dear, Lord" and "Amen" during the congregational prayer, or "long" prayer, present the best time to sneak in a nap. Long periods of singing also offer a good opportunity to make some noise and stretch our legs. A short snack, usually a Wilhelmina peppermint, comes just before the message, and our eyes lock on the clock to see how long it will last before it dissolves under the indomitable forces of our saliva.

We invent several silent, secret games to occupy our minds as well. It's in church that I hone my counting skills. We count organ pipes, ceiling tiles, window squares, comb-overs, and bald heads. For the more advanced mathematicians, we discover a diverse range of opportunities to play with the numbers listed on the song boards, which we slice up, add, subtract, multiply, and divide. Sometimes we race to find the longest song in the blue Psalter Hymnal, or the shortest. In moments of forced stillness, the mind sometimes runs wild, so the natural byproduct of this weekly hour of stillness is the development of a fantastic imagination in us kids.

Sundays, in general, are a muddled day of rest. We are allowed to see our cousins at our grandparents' house after church for cookies and coffee, but playing with them after that point is considered a sin. Riding our bikes used to be a Sabbath violation when we were younger but eventually

God changed his mind about that and we were given permission to ride, though still not with our cousins, of course.

Many Christians participate in a perpetually heated debate if it's acceptable to eat out on Sunday. With my family, though, there's no room for dispute on this issue: it is definitely not permitted, with absolutely no exceptions. It would be a terrible violation to force someone else to work on the mandatory day of rest, unless one is on vacation, and then, of course, God understands.

As more and more businesses in town open their doors on Sunday, we of the Christian Reformed churches shake our heads in repugnance. What is happening to the world? Oh, the calamity! The revoltingly offensive total depravity! This issue produces a holy anger that demands speaking up. Insurrection time. Time to march through the streets wearing sandwich boards declaring the wrath of God upon those who visit these establishments on the holy day of rest (unless of course, it's an out-of-state license plate—they must be on vacation). Time to ban the restaurants who value profit above God! Okay, so we never actually march down the streets of Holland, but we occasionally blast an indignant letter to the editor of the Holland Sentinel.

I must confess, though, I love getting all dressed up in my Sunday best, or "church clothes" as we call them. I especially need to look good because our family always shows up late and is subsequently ushered to the very front of church. It's a fashion runway show of sorts. I always make sure to truss up my long, thick hair in all sorts of whimsical ways. At our church, everyone always looks good, and everyone is always doing good.

Typical Sunday morning conversation. "Hi." *Handshake.* "How are you?"

"Good. How are you?" *Big smile.*

"Good." *Big smile back.*

"Good."

Beneath this picture-perfect, polished veneer of goodness, beneath the professionally bleached-white toothy smiles, beneath the exterior religious ritual, lurks a deeply held assumption that we have a theology superior to all others. We have a perfect unerring outline of all things pertaining to God, and we are quick and confident to point out the condemning flaws of all the others outside of our theological sphere. Ironically, even though our Reformed theology professes that we're all sinners, rarely it seems, does any of us *actually* sin. Church is a funny place like that.

Every once in a while, a few absolutely known exceptionally sinful sinners pepper our perfect congregation, such as the occasional pregnant teenager who stands before the congregation shackled to her shame, confessing that she has been bonked by a boy. Never mind the role of the boy. Never mind that many Christian high schoolers bonk in the back of their cars just like the public school kids. I sometimes wonder if the sin is not so much the bonking as it is the getting caught bonking.

In my hometown of Holland, Michigan, people say that there is a church on every street corner. Actually, two churches inhabit every street corner: the Christian Reformed Church (CRC) and across from it, inevitably, a Reformed Church of America (RCA). The two denominations have a history of competing to be seated at the right hand of God. Ironically, the differences between the two today are so minuscule, you'd need a trained eye and a microscope to pick them out. No doubt, members of both will walk through the pearly gates, but only one will be seated at God's right hand, and the other will have to settle for his left.

Historically, we used to be one denomination, but over time various issues divided us into separate church bodies. The CRC (my tribe) broke away from the RCA for several reasons. The RCA began allowing all believers in Jesus to partake of communion, while the CRC insisted on members with approved membership papers only, just like Jesus did. Also, the RCA allowed hymns in worship, but the CRC exclusively limited its singing to the Psalms. The RCA let the mother tongue (Dutch) slip away, encouraging and embracing the English language, a very slippery slope towards embracing "worldly" American culture, with all its dancing and card-playing. The CRC folks clung rigorously to the Dutch language, the suspected original language of the blond-haired, blue-eyed Jesus, whose picture hangs in our Sunday School room.

But eventually, even the CRC came around to utilizing the English language. Card-playing and dancing inevitably followed, though a truly committed member of the CRC limits his/her dancing to the Dutch Shuffle, which basically involves shifting one's weight from one leg to the other and back again. In fact, not only did we eventually embrace the language and much of the American culture, but we later went on to mandate that same culture we formerly abhorred as we spread the gospel "message" to the various tribes of Native Americans across the land. In order to be followers of Jesus, we insisted that they talk like us, dress like us, style their hair like us and take on all our other "civilized" manners.

Other differences between the denominations developed over time. The CRC strongly encouraged parents to consider a Christian education—kindergarten through twelfth grade—to give their children a more thorough indoctrination of the Reformed perspective so they could defend their faith when thrust out into the world. Meanwhile, the RCA suggested that students attend public schools. The RCA allowed parishioners to be members of lodges, but the CRC folks limited its people to hold a membership in their church exclusively. And, of course, the Republican Party. From what I can tell, the RCA has encouraged engagement with the world, while the CRC has tended to exhibit a separatist purity, just as God mandated.

In this small world in which I live, I can tell you with conclusiveness that, despite our similarities, we—the CRC—are more right than the RCA. There is a reason, after all, why we are called the *Christian* Reformed Church.

We focus on getting our theological ducks in a row, not only to get to heaven, but also to gain confidence in divulging and defending what we believe. Over the course of my early life, a clay pot of sorts is molded and filled. Molded by the hands of the Christian Reformed Church and filled with the soil of the theology of John Calvin and his fellow Reformers. I am the seed that has been planted and nurtured in the soil of this pot. I have slowly emerged through the surface, a tender sprout. As my roots crawl down and tangle with the soil, I begin to grow and await the blooming. My worldview—all the neat and tidy answers to the questions of the universe—makes up the nutrients sustaining my growth in the confines of my pretty little clay pot.

Occasionally, someone asks me a question that I've never thought about, and I don't have a pre-constructed, tidy retort. But like a suave presidential candidate in a televised debate, I soon become crafty at steering those responses to one of my prescribed and practiced answers, regardless of whether it has anything to do with the question. Throwing in a few intelligent theological terms or catch phrases always adds to my air of confidence and illusion of superiority on the subject.

There is no need to think for myself or to seek out the meaning of Scripture on my own because someone has already done the work for me, rather like a doctor prescribing medicine to a compliant patient who has no idea what is in the medicine. In fact, our church teachers and pastors often convey the dangers of one's own search for meaning. The word "dangerous" is like a mantra in our tradition. To read material that holds a view contrary to our absolute and final resolutions? Dangerous. To pose questions outside of the prescribed questions? Dangerous. The soil outside of my pot? Absolutely dangerous.

Somehow, these great European theologians of long ago got it all exactly figured out. Very few in the history of the world before or since have had anything substantial to add or subtract to their "rightness." Perhaps John Calvin was the second Coming of Christ. I have wondered about that. Maybe the Holy Spirit isn't vigorously rolling through our church because he has nothing new to teach us since we are spot on in all our conclusions. And what if the Holy Spirit teaches us something contrary to John Calvin? This would cause a real quandary. A very *dangerous* quandary, indeed.

We view all Scripture through the lens of our theology. Rarely does anyone ask: "Is this biblically accurate?" On the other hand, I often hear someone ask: "Is this theologically accurate?" And if anyone does ask if something is biblically accurate, he or she is basically asking whether or not it is biblically accurate *according to Reformed theology.*

Perhaps the focus on nailing down our theology so completely stems from the idea of being saved by grace, through faith, rather than by good works. The Philippian jailer asked the apostle Paul what must he do to be saved, and Paul responds, "Believe in the Lord Jesus and you will be saved." Thus, our tradition emphasizes what we *believe* rather than what we do—which completely separates us from "those Catholics" who try to save themselves through good works. Since we deem our actions largely irrelevant, we need to *believe* the right things (though I'm pretty sure believing counts as *doing* something). Having correct knowledge is key to being saved, and this correct Reformed understanding of Scripture is hammered into us through song, sermon, Sunday school, and Christian private schooling.

In high school, I attend the Young Calvinist Convention, a week-long annual summer gathering of thousands of Christian Reformed high school kids from across the country. We all unite in solidarity behind John Calvin's brilliant summarization of all things pertaining to God. It's basically a big melting pot of hyper-excited hormonal teenagers, mainly of common Dutch ancestry. I'll just say the gene pool runs pretty shallow. Approximately 150 years prior, our forefathers emigrated from the

Netherlands and settled in pockets all over the United States and Canada. In these communities our ancestors multiplied like wild rabbits, so the convention is basically one big annual family reunion of a singular generation, several times removed.

Every night of the convention, we participate in something called the hug line. The girls stretch in a line across the campus, while the boys come through in a procession and hug us. Since the usual Christian Reformed greeting is a stiff handshake, I speculate that this ritual is the denomination's subtle way of encouraging denominational inbreeding, a surefire way to encourage a new generation of purebred Dutch Calvinists. The boys walk down the line, check the girls out—examine the meat, so to speak—and mentally make their selections to pursue throughout the week. Okay, so I can't say this is what goes on in the boys' heads for sure, but it certainly has the potential to be that. As one of the girls, it certainly feels like that. I do know of at least one match made at one of these conventions that flourished. They went on to produce three blond-haired, blue-eyed Calvinists of their own, absolute purebreds.

The first time I went to convention, it was held in Edmonton, Alberta. Every convention promises a fun day away. In Edmonton, the day away meant a trip to the biggest mall in North America, complete with an indoor water park. I savored the opportunity to travel to a foreign country (if Canada can be considered such) as well as to do some serious shopping with my girlfriends from church. I had no idea what was coming.

Here, for the first time, I am exposed to inspirational speakers—speakers who seem to communicate in a way that connects with me—and singing all sorts of praise music, music that is definitely not in our church hymn book. People lift their hands in the air and sometimes tears fall—like nothing I have ever experienced at my church before.

Back at home it's all serious, straight-faced hymn singing. Most people sing with an expression on their face that says, "I'm constipated," or as if they are mentally scratching up the next week's to-do list. While the occasional person truly and obviously sings from her soul, many simply look like architects standing before a conference room full of half-asleep board members, presenting plans for an elevator in a factory building. This way of worshiping is the Dutch-American Christian Reformed way, also known as God's way, or *the* way.

Yet here I sit at the convention, hearing speakers talk with conviction, in a language and tone that resonates well with me, and with a passionate gusto I have never heard before. Masses of kids and chaperones sing songs of praise and lament, their whole being rhythmically sways to the pounding beat. I can't believe the loss of emotional control I feel as my voice joins in the chorus with all the others. It's as if some invisible hand has reached into my heart and squeezed it with such a force that it coerces a stampede of liquid from my tear ducts. All this, over God, Jesus, the Holy Spirit. What is happening here?

It's the first time I have ever really felt—what I assume to be—the Holy Spirit. This feeling surges through my veins and pierces my heart. I know all *about* the Holy Spirit, I can dissect him and cite chapter and verse about him, but I have never actually *experienced* the Holy Spirit. Feeling so persuaded and intoxicated by this Spirit, I find myself ethereally swept up to the front of the masses in response to the altar call, fallen on my knees, and offering my life up for service to the one who offered his life to me.

But when the music stops and the adults shuffle us back to our dorm rooms, I lie wide awake with my head on my pillow, staring into darkness—confused and full of questions. *Did I betray my faith by being at the altar, committing my life to Christ? Haven't I already done that? Haven't I already received my once-and-for-all ticket to heaven?* I toss and turn, contemplating: *Did Jesus have to memorize the Heidelberg Catechism? Did his disciples? Did they have a golden certificate mounted on their bedroom wall, as I do?*

Then a number of *perhaps* start flowing through my mind: *Perhaps faith isn't that complicated; perhaps it isn't such a formal perfunctory, prescribed procedure. Perhaps it's just a decision you make, something your heart says yes to and you follow through by how you live your life. Perhaps our "public profession of faith" is the way we live out our faith, not a single service at which we make a few statements, say "I do" to a few questions. Perhaps my whole life should be a testimony to my faith.* I leave the week feeling somewhat confused.

A couple of my friends and I decide to be Righteous Renegades in our church when we return home from our first convention. We want to stir things up a little, put some *pizazz* in worship, perform some critical acts of CPR to the Holy Spirit—certain that if we blow a little life into the nostrils of the Holy Ghost, his power will flow from us and eventually ignite even the pious, purple-haired ladies sitting so stoically in the rear pews.

We hatch a brilliant little plan, involving banding together for a Sunday service and lifting our hands to the heavens, our bodies pendulating as we sing out with deep down fervor. Surely it will catch on, will spread easily like creamy butter on bread straight from the oven so that even the porous surface of the old wooden sanctuary will absorb this smack of delightful Holy Ghost goodness. It will be a moment never forgotten, like the emotional climax of a Hallmark card commercial. Someday they will be saying, "Remember when the Holy Spirit came to church? Remember how it so filled and moved us that we who experienced it would rather go to the grave then back to the old way of worshipping?" Yes, this is what they will be saying.

When the service arrived and the plan was underway, we find ourselves squirming inside as we try desperately to force inspiration upon ourselves. Then I think: *What has happened to me? I've never questioned the superiority of the pipe organ.* But now it seems so ancient—slowly blowing air through the pipes like a fat man out cold on a rickety old lounge chair, snoring, with one hand hooked in his shorts and an empty, crumpled up beer can unconsciously clamped in the other. The organ actually stifles the inspiration in me. Suddenly, our faces begin passing through all shades of red, realizing how absolutely ridiculous and out of place we feel in the church we've been attending our entire lives. I intensely try to force excitement, so much so that it's physically painful. An onerous feeling looms over me in this place now that I've experienced a different way of "doing" church.

And, to be frank, it's just plain unnatural to raise your hands to the singing of "Blest Be the Tie That Binds," accompanied by a bellowing organ, aka the snoring fat man, than it is to "Shine Jesus Shine," accompanied by a band complete with electric guitars, a drum set, and background vocals. But the three of us had made a pact to keep our arms raised through all the verses of the song, and we remain true to our word. Meanwhile, confused eyes stare at us, probably wondering if we're grasping at little fuzzies in the air, highlighted by the shafts of the day's remaining light streaming though the tall sanctuary windows. It's just our luck that the organ blows slowly through every single stanza on this particular occasion.

"Okay, so that was awkward," my friends and I agree. It seems that just as quickly as the Holy Spirit has taken up residence in my life, he disappears. This is the way worship has been done for over a hundred years. They say, "You can't teach an old dog new tricks," and apparently they are right. But also, perhaps sometimes the old dog just needs to be left alone. I'm beginning to learn a thing or two about subcultural context.

~ ~ ~

As I enter my sophomore year of high school, a new passion begins to stir within me, but I'm unsure what to do with it, and I'm quite certain the devil is mixed up in it somewhere. In my inability to dissolve this ever-lurking desire, I embrace it, and it instead becomes my secret sin. It becomes a great darkness that my heart silently and persistently yearns to leap for, to grasp onto, to embrace. It is the deep down yearning to communicate the message of Jesus to the broken world, from behind the pulpit. Yes, from *behind* the pulpit.

Well aware that a woman becoming a preacher would be a sin, a direct disobedience to God Most High, I keep my desire tucked deeply in the back of my cranium. Yet the pull towards the pulpit, the aching want of it, becomes so strong that I can't possibly set it aside and ignore it. I begin carrying a small note pad around with me at all times and jot down the sermon illustrations that I now find everywhere in life. No one will suspect, with its worn, sky-blue cover, that this notebook contains the musings of a wanna-be woman pastor.

Eventually I dare myself to write whole sermons, and they begin coming to me faster than I can scribe them into my new, larger, red spiral-bound notebook. I write "Subject: chemistry" on the cover in permanent black marker and also doodle a smattering of comical little faces in order to camouflage it. I cling to it like a German spy would his notes, hoping no one ever suspects its condemning contents. I pray that God, whom I know sees beyond the cover, will somehow take my secret desire to be silly schoolgirl sentiments, a harmless little make-believe. I stay up late into the nights with a flashlight under the covers, my pen working overtime.

We all draw lines of ethics and morality, lines we tell ourselves we will never cross. But now I find myself at the edge of this moral line, which must not be crossed, and so I continue to push and stretch it farther and farther outward. Since I keep the sermons to myself, I decide that God will forgive me. The sin would be in the actual preaching, after all.

But in time, I feel as if I will burst with my secret, and so I set up a pulpit, a tree stump actually, deep in the woods behind the farm in a great cathedral of maple trees and other hardwoods, where shafts of sunlight pour in from above. I preach with conviction, all the poetic outpourings my mind can muster. To the trees, the red squirrels, the bluegill in the pond, and all the other unseen microscopic critters that abound in a forest,

I creatively tell of God's majesty, his irresistible grace, and every other point of Scripture that fits within the confines of our inerrant theology. Eventually, whole worship services, complete with hymns and prayers, take place in my clandestine, outdoor, mossy church—nature alone in attendance. I rationalize, find my loophole: *I am within the grasp of God's grace because I am not preaching to any sort of creatures with actual souls.*

But all this stretching of moral boundaries sits heavy on my conscience, and sleepless nights ensue. I so love to study God's word and feel called to preach it. But I wonder: *How much do I really know and love Him, if in the way I desire to tell others about Him, I directly disobey Him? Would God ever forgive me? If I one day pursue preaching, which I know would be wrong of me to do, will I be more of a stumbling block than a blessing to those around me? Will my words be from the devil, even though they are of God? Or could God possibly use me to bring others to Him, even in and through my sin-soaked method?* This plants a new question within me: *Would I actually be willing to preach the gospel to the world, personally risking the eternal blazes of Hell in order to spare others from that kind of suffering?* These questions plague me.

I devour and relish every opportunity to be behind the real pulpit in the acceptable, non-preacher roles. I begin feeding the congregation updates on the various activities of our church youth group. I also jump at the chance to deliver compelling speeches regarding various mission projects in which I've taken part, or to address our congregation on the ways in which I've benefitted from some spiritual retreat. I start singing solos on a regular basis in worship. Every moment behind the pulpit provides small bits of sustenance to the starving preacher-creature within me.

During my junior year of high school, I enroll in speech class. I, of course, take advantage of the opportunity and manipulate every type of required speech into some sort of sermon. After the speakers finish, the class members give required feedback. The feedback I receive contains encouragement (from the RCA kids, no doubt) to be a preacher. I secretly start to wonder if I am adopted and my real birth parents are actually generational RCA members. Or maybe, because the CRC came out of the RCA, some genetics from the distant RCA relatives may have lain dormant, silently passing themselves on through the generations and now suddenly have decided to express themselves in my genetic makeup. I trace this genetic abnormality to the fact of my being born in sin. *Hmmm*, I think, *this could be an effective sermon illustration examining the consequences of humanity's fallen nature.* I scratch the idea down in my notepad.

Every year I look forward to parent-teacher conferences at school because my teachers always report to my parents that my spiritual maturity ranks well above average. A nice pat on the back for me. I have a deep sense that I'm a better Christian than most of the others in my school since I don't swear, don't drink, never attend R-rated movies, and—to top it off—I speak up about my concern for those who do, despite being an introvert. I also listen exclusively to the Christian radio station and shop at the local Christian bookstore for cute little cross-laden trinkets or "holy hardware," as a friend of mine refers to such items.

Never mind my swelling pride. Never mind the judgmental attitude I have toward my classmates. Never mind the fact that I'm quickly blossoming into a first-class, stubborn, spiritual narcissist. By all appearances, I'm the girl other parents wish theirs to be like, which only pumps further air in my growing, unseen self-righteousness. Within me a sort of rot spreads slowly, creeping in quietly, though it will be several years before I become aware of this reality.

There's another key component to my worldview: politics. In my community, a tight marriage between Christianity and the Republican Party exists. Our church members frown upon divorce of these two forces, or even a temporary separation. Anyone who strays from the Right can hardly be considered a follower of Jesus. To criticize a Republican president would be like slapping the face of Jesus. In fact, I'm pretty sure that Jesus rode an elephant into Jerusalem on Passover. A donkey would have certainly been unclean! Rush Limbaugh, Pat Buchanan, and George Will roll off the tongue as common household names, right up there with John Calvin, Abraham Kuyper, and Jesus Christ.

The political stance seems to boil down to one main issue: abortion. The sanctity of life. Life is precious, mostly so before birth. We all know that Democrats want to kill babies yet unborn, and Republicans want to save them. I have seen enough photos of burned, chopped up, half-developed babies, enough images of pieces of little baby arms, legs, and torsos in trash cans to know that the Democrats are the devil, which automatically makes anything they say evil, twisted, and untrustworthy. Any positions they take that appear to lean toward good are simply deceitful tricks, seductive talking points to distract us while they continue the slaughter.

One day in the fall of my senior year, our history teacher prompts a class discussion on the upcoming presidential election. It's Clinton/Gore vs. Bush/Quayle. I wonder what can possibly be up for discussion. Republican vs. Democrat, Good vs. Evil. And then, cutting into all my wondering, a girl in my class speaks up in support of the Democratic Party and their concern for the poor. I am shocked! Aghast! I can almost see the devil sitting on her shoulder, red fork in hand, whispering in her ear, and sweetly calling her to come hither—like the sneaky serpent in the garden.

Good grief, I think, *Bill Clinton is the anti-Christ. Hasn't she been reading her Bible?* It was a given that Jesus was a staunch Republican. Like us, Jesus knew that the best way to help the poor was by ignoring them so they would get motivated to pull themselves up by their own sandal straps. We all know that. We all know that those black-hearted Democrats are eager to rip every ripe baby from the womb and torture it. How is this girl so unaware? No doubt she is a Catholic, or heaven forbid, a member of the Reformed Church. My head dramatically swings from side to side at the thought of her foul, reprehensible ideas.

I lean over and whisper to my friend across the aisle. "That's heresy." I shake my head. "She needs Jesus."

Our mission as disciples of Jesus is to tell more people about Jesus so they can get to heaven too. When life gets wearisome, we can assure them that things will be unimaginably resplendent in the life to come. We will one day walk through the pearly gates, in our perfectly healthy Christie Brinkley bodies, up the streets of gold, beside the sea of crystal, to our very own mansions of glory, complete with glistening underground pools and professionally-landscaped yards. One of my pastors once said that when we open our mouths to sing in the choir with the angels, perfect three-part harmonies will come out of every individual. I always thought that would be pretty cool, though I did secretly wonder in the back of my mind why, then, heaven would need a choir at all. But I knew better than to raise the question. I also wondered how he got that bit of information. Perhaps he discovered some secret, classified journal of the late John Calvin. But again, no questions asked.

The alternative is to go down, down, down to a place of eternal torment, to be swallowed by eternal flames that will constantly lick our bodies with smoldering tongues, without ever completely consuming us, which will—fittingly—hurt like hell. It's a no-brainer really.

When opportunities arise (and I am always on the lookout for them), I can easily present the gospel in five minutes, like a smooth door-to-door salesman, on a napkin or an old receipt fished from the bottom of my purse. I have two particularly favorite ways to explain the gospel message. First, the Bridge Diagram. I draw two cliffs with an adjoining bridge and proceed to explain how YOU stand on one cliff while GOD stands on the other cliff, and the cross of Jesus bridges the gap, providing a way to cross over the yawning chasm of hell.

For the more detail-oriented recipients, I find the T.U.L.I.P. acronym more appropriate. Here's the breakdown of T.U.L.I.P., also known as *The Five Points of Calvinism*:

1. Total Depravity: We are born sinners, destined for an eternity in hell. Every aspect of our being is tainted with sinfulness—every thought, deed, motive, etc.

2. Unconditional Election: God chooses who he wants to get into heaven. There is nothing I can do to win his favor. Nothing I can do to gain entry into heaven. Nothing. It's not a matter of what I want, but of what he wants.

3. Limited Atonement: Jesus died only for the elect (members of the CRC), only for those he chose. Though his sacrifice was efficient for all, it was not efficacious for all.

4. Irresistible Grace: When God calls his elect into salvation, they cannot resist. God offers to all people the gospel message. But as for the elect (especially members of the CRC), they are powerless to refuse it.

5. Perseverance of the saints: You cannot lose your salvation. Once you have been saved, you are always saved. There is no turning back. Eternal security in Christ.

Basically, T.U.L.I.P. boils down to this: Unless you're part of the Jesus fraternity, you will burn in hell. You just better hope God is in a good mood when your name comes up for consideration when he's inscribing names into the Book of Life. Otherwise, you're screwed. Actually, come to think of it, his mood doesn't matter—he made up his mind a long time ago. There is nothing you can do. He has already decided who is "in" and who is "out," and you are powerless to accept or refuse it. You're handed either heaven or hell by this good and loving God.

If the recipient of my T.U.L.I.P. presentation looks puzzled, I echo exactly what others have confirmed to me: "Yes, it makes God seem crass, but sometimes God just doesn't make sense to our limited human mental capabilities."

Then I give the classic example—as if this solves the whole "God is good but intentionally condemns people to eternal hell" problem—putting Mother Theresa side-by-side with Adolf Hitler. I explain: "Both are sinful to the core. Mother Theresa sacrificed her entire life to care for some of the most decrepitly wretched existences of humanity the world has ever known, but she is Catholic and therefore certainly bound for an eternity of fire and brimstone because she depended on her works to save her soul. On the other hand, Hitler, sympathetic to Protestant theology, may well have had a "Come-to-Jesus" moment, which would make him saved by grace and residing in eternal tropical utopia with an all-you-can-eat poolside buffet. You might expect the opposite, but it just goes to show that sometimes God's ways are not our ways.

However, there is a shred of hope. If you embrace the five points of T.U.L.I.P., then the odds are in your favor. If you are of Dutch decent, the odds definitely fall in your favor. If you have memorized at least 10% of the Heidelberg Catechism, the odds are slightly in your favor. If you regularly pull the lever for the Republican ticket, the odds are distinctly in your favor. If you have done three or more of the above, consider yourself in the club. And if you are Christian Reformed by blood or conversion, those credentials automatically secure you a membership in heaven."

The whole thing is just so obvious to me—it's incomprehensible as to why the whole world doesn't want to join the CRC. The message of salvation is so simple.

And my closing statement usually goes something like this: "Just say *yes* to the plan, do the memory work, sign on the dotted line, and you're in. You will be issued a beautiful certificate to mount on your wall. Just a few small things to keep in mind, though. Try to stay clear of swearing, dirty dancing, having sex outside of marriage, or going to R-rated movies. Never ask dangerous questions. Be sure to get to a Christian Reformed church every week, twice if you can. Congratulations on getting in the club! I'll see you in heaven. Perhaps our mansions will be in the same gated subdivision. Wouldn't that be something? Oh, and don't forget to pick up your George Bush bumper sticker."

Boom. Another soul saved.

CHAPTER THREE

Uprooted

THEY CALL ME "JACKIE O" on Capitol Hill. Despite being on the other side of the political aisle and not exactly a *fashionista*, I'm somehow swept away by former Jacqueline Kennedy Onassis' style. She was magical, timelessly classy. My adoration for her leaves me poring over coffee table picture books of her, and then trailing off to antique stores in hopes of finding the big black glasses and cute little suit dresses just like hers. In time, I can't even bring myself to pick up a loaf of bread at the grocery store without donning a darling little sundress and matching sandals.

I've mentioned it before—but this point is critical and really can't be overstated enough, so pay attention: Where I come from, all Republicans are *not* necessarily Christians, but all Christians *are* necessarily Republicans. If you support any other political party, we pretty much assume that you have the number 666 stamped and hidden somewhere on your body. So I, in turn, have always understood that anyone who exerts himself for the Republican Party, not only gains a speed pass to the seventh level of heaven, but is pretty much guaranteed a reserved seat at the right hand of God.

It was with this in mind that I graduated from Calvin College with a B.A. in Political Science, in 1999. After proudly walking across the stage to receive my diploma, I headed to Washington D.C. with my head held high, taking a job with a Republican congressman. I couldn't have felt prouder or more important because I was now one of God's footmen on this planet, promoting his policies in the most practical ways.

Currently, the Republicans control the House and the Democrats control the Senate. Bill Clinton serves in his second term as president, and although he admits his involvement is inappropriate, he "did not have sex with that woman, Miss Lewinsky." Upon further independent investigations, it has been brought to the world's attention that many of the politicians who called for Clinton's resignation are guilty of their own sexual affairs, which ought not to surprise anyone really. Welcome to Washington D.C.

My job on the Hill is fairly insignificant. I'm basically a glorified receptionist with a few other responsibilities. Nevertheless, I take great pleasure in being counted among the lucky few who get to serve one of these Jesus-men in office. I will gladly be a martyr in slicing open that package stamped "fragile" with a mini bomb inside, if it will save the congressman. Like Mary, I will rub oil over his feet with my hair, if the opportunity presents itself.

The atmosphere constantly sprinkles down a tangible air of importance that one feels in this city. Hordes of important people bustle to their important places to do in their important jobs. I immediately absorb this self-importance on day one of the job. In the very moment I adorn myself with a fitted black suit and slip on a pair of black heels, it all screams "Important!" I feel beyond grown up. Here I am in the midst of this ridiculously fast-paced city, with my chin a notch higher than usual, and everything about my surroundings and demeanor confirms my self-importance. Even transferring from one packed Metro to another, from one crammed escalator to the next, all become subtle reminders to me that I have grown up. I have grown up and become so important.

It's impressive to daily walk alongside people I've only seen interviewed on CNN or plastered on the front page of the *Washington Post*. And I'm eminently flattered to be noticed by more than one of these gods with their little congressional gold pins stuck firmly in their suit jackets. The flirtations on their behalf are due, in large part, to my polished Jackie O charm, no doubt. I feel indomitable, pompously walking past these strong men, with my confident head held high, knowing they cannot have what their eyes desire, knowing that it is I who hold the power in these scenarios.

The pay is tolerable, but the perks are great. Evenings often involve receptions hosted by one big corporation or another, in an attempt to keep good relations with the politicians and their staff. These frequent opportunities for Congress to be in bed—both figuratively and literally—with big business are critical. It's important in the game of "You scratch my back, I'll scratch yours," sometimes called "You pass the legislation I want, and I'll provide the funds to get you reelected," but more commonly referred to as simply "American politics." I was quick to learn that this is the way the game works—in stark contrast to the textbook version which tends to romanticize our American democracy. And if you want to be in the game, you have to play by the rules.

This is the reality of the way American democracy, coupled with crony capitalism, works. Money equals speech. No money, no speech. (Know money, know speech?) Any individual working in Washington, or any American paying attention at all, for that matter, would have to have a thick veil over their eyes not to see it. But what can I do about it? The system is too big, the corruption too embedded for one person to make any significant changes. And so I position myself in the game and play.

Despite the real motives behind these after-work receptions, as a staff person, they're great opportunities to mingle and network with other congressional staff persons, and to get a delectable free dinner. Cooking for one tends to get repetitive, so free dinners are important for the mass of us single twenty- and thirty-something's running the show, writing legislation, and doing all the footwork while the congresspersons focus on making newsworthy appearances, back-scratching, and getting re-elected.

Besides these obvious frivolities, I find engrossing satisfaction in daily passing by the great monuments constructed in honor of once-great men, ascending the steps into the congressional buildings of the now-great men and women, and walking the towering marble-lined hallways to my cozy office nook. Even going through metal detectors on a daily basis provides a sweet measure of gratification because it all tells me that I'm important. Every day these reminders subtly whisper that I am part of something great, something big.

But a very real and very converse reality lurks just outside those doors, just near the bottom of the steps that daily ascend my vainglory: The home-less. The destitute. The crack-head prostitutes. Just. Outside. My. Door.

The sight of these stinking people, swaddled in rags, is like a one-two punch to my stomach. Coming from rolling farm country, my eyes have never glimpsed anything quite like it, at least not in America, the wealthi-est nation in the world. I spent some time in Asia a few years ago and recall the streets of Indonesia littered with desperation—children cooling off in the open sewers, mothers nearly tearing my clothes off as part of their begging ritual. But this is Washington D.C., the pulsating heartbeat of America, the place of power, prestige, and cash flowing like the waters of the Potomac at flood stage. I was not expecting so much poverty and filth to lie in these streets and parks named after great American presidents and successful military leaders, a string of them connecting the many great memorials to the Greek architectural columns that house the many governmental offices. I'm sometimes nauseated by the sound of their begging cries.

Oh. My. God.

Beggars. Real people. Not some hobo on a movie screen. Not a scene from one of those New York City cop shows. Poverty, hunger, the stench of liquor, and the closeness of death actually unfold before me in real time, in real flesh and blood. Right at my Jackie O heels. I can see them with my actual eyes. I can sometimes taste them when I flit by and their thick stench wafts through the air, chases me down, and assaults me. It's unnerving. I'm entirely lost on what to do. It's so foreign to my existence that I don't even have a clue as to how I'm supposed to feel about it all, what I'm supposed to think.

Shortly after my arrival, I begin asking several friends and colleagues about the stench of poverty on the outside of our air-conditioned world. I wonder how they cope with this visible brokenness day after day. It feels like a daily walk through hell to get to our little slice of heaven. Most give formulaic responses: "You'll get used to it. Everyone does. Soon you won't even see those drunk bastards anymore." A few suggest volunteering at a reputable nonprofit organization that has a screening process so that only the homeless "worthy of help" can get help. And nearly always comes the suggestion that I should never give handouts of any sort because I will only encourage their laziness. Inevitably, as a closing remark to seal their argument, comes the reminder that the important work I'm doing for my Republican congressman is their real, true, and lasting hope.

They're right. Of course they're right. In some complicated way unknown to me, they must be right. They are God's angels on earth, after all. And I do want to help these desperate people in a real, true, and lasting way. So like a spanking, it seems cruel to briskly breeze past them, but in time they will learn the hard lesson, that in order to survive, they must sober up and get a job. It's that simple. And so ignore them I do. On my Jackie O heels, I promenade on past.

~ ~ ~

After only six weeks on the job, a study tour to Israel interrupts the D.C. high life. I am assigned a hearty list of required Scripture readings and several historical facts and time periods to memorize before the trip, and I decide to take advantage of the daily stillness on the Metro to get in my reading. I squirm a little inside, sitting with my nose in my travel Bible, while the rest of the Metro commuters—mostly important people, no doubt—sit immersed in the daily newspapers. I find myself feeling embarrassed, wanting to mask my Bible with the pages of the *Washington Post*, much the same way Davy Vander Cragt used to hide a comic book in his history textbook during our seventh grade U.S. history class.

But the biggest dilemma for me in preparation for the trip: What would Jackie wear rambling over the terrain of the Middle East? The glasses are a no-brainer.

Chapter Four

A Slight Fracture

Our driver, Chaim, maneuvers the bus like Wile E. Coyote, swerving up and down hills and around bends through the desert in Israel. Gripping the seat, I half expect we'll engage in a sloppy wet kiss with the rock wall on one side, or plunge the dreadful depths of the cliff on the other side, lacking the advantage of repetitive comeback that the coyote always seems to miraculously pull off. Without warning, we pull off the road at what absolutely does not look like a tourist destination. Our indefatigable leader on this journey hops off the bus and is off like a shot. He is a teacher with a fire in his chest, having led countless groups on similar study tours. "Come, let's go," he says, eager to share his passion for studying the text in its context. And in the flip of a pancake, he is gone. We all clamor to get off the bus in a frantic effort to keep up with this lion.

Our group hoofs it through the scorching desert, dust kicking up with every stride, never knowing where we're headed. Each journey's end is never revealed until we're on the spot. I suppose each moment is an end in and of itself. "It's as much about the journey as it is about the destination," our leader keeps saying, and we're expected to make the most of every moment. I have tremendous respect for our leader, who also happens to have been my high school Bible teacher, as well as a spiritual mentor throughout those years. I decide I will trust him on this excursion and cautiously open myself up to new possibilities.

As my aching feet pound miles of this parched and thirsty shard of earth, I notice with curiosity the clusters of sheep and shepherds dotting the hills here and there—rolling mounds of crusty terrain as barren as a monkey's rump. What kind of unsparing punishment are these sheep being subjected to? PETA would pitch a fit!

Suddenly we stop. On a hillside we stop. Edging the crack of the monkey's rump, we stop. I'm guessing this location must be our objective because pausing for breaks hasn't been typical on this trip so far. And so I'm wondering, *What could be so noteworthy about this place? We have traversed a dozen identical bone-dry hillsides on our way to this one.* But again, it's never just about the destination; it's about the journey as well.

Our leader's typically booming voice finds its way into my exhausted mind with the words of Psalm 23: "The Lord is my Shepherd, I shall not be in want. He makes me lie down in green pastures…" These familiar words come to me anew, shimmying their way through me, from naval to nose. His hands extend wide, indicating barren land stretching itself far and wide. "These are the green pastures. You're sitting in what the Bible refers to as 'green pastures,'" he tells us. We're dispensed a few moments of silence to let that take hold.

My jaw falls and a bit of dust blows past my dry lips and sticks to my teeth. But this small annoyance is nothing compared to the irritation I feel at this new understanding of "green pastures." *Is this what it's all about then?* I wonder, starting to feel a little disturbed. In fact, I find I'm actually borderline angry. I've been duped. Here I've been all these years, seeking comfort in the words of Psalm 23, imagining God walking beside me through endless acres of South Dakota prairie grass, expanding into the horizon beneath a bottomless blue sky. The exhalation of his intoxicating, balmy, sweet breath sending rolling, mesmerizing waves over the unblemished green grasses of forever. But now, my ravishing illusions adjourn as I imagine God, instead, hurling me into the middle of a desert when I'm at my worst.

I cross my arms, furrow my brow. Petulance is brewing and bubbling within me. Before embitterment solders itself to my bones, the clarifying explanation comes. It turns out that on certain sides of the hills, during specific times of the day, moisture collects under the little rocks strewn over the hills. This dampness gathers enough weight to drop itself to the ground and a couple sprigs of grass grow on the thirsty, but extremely fertile, patch of earth, suckling the millimeter of shade beside the rock. The shepherd knows when and where to graze the sheep. The sheep totally depend on their shepherd to lead them day-by-day to the food they need. If they wander from his voice, they will die. The sheep always have enough if they follow the shepherd—never an abundance—but always and only enough.

The point is that God will provide. He never assures us a cornucopia. He promises enough for each day, as long as we hear his voice and follow. Enough grace, enough patience, enough endurance, enough hope, enough of all that we need to get through life day by day. God simplifying our needs—a revolutionary concept to me. Who knew that such a subtle change in word pictures could so portentously restyle my understanding of God?

The spindles in my head begin to churn as I recall the Israelites roaming the desert collecting just enough manna for today, every day. There, too, God promised he would provide just enough for that day, and he did. That which they hoarded turned to rot. *Green pastures, I ponder,* in a different light. The words continue to inhabit my mind and, slowly from there, penetrate my heart.

I begin to reflect on the ramifications of this revelation: *How does this apply to me in twentieth-century America, where over-abundance is the norm and wants have morphed into needs?* I can't give the cold shoulder to the question that keeps obstinately resurfacing as we pick up and continue to graze our aching feet through the desert: *How much do I really depend on God for my needs? And what of all the excess?* I mean, I work so I can get a paycheck and buy all that I need and much of what I want. I have health insurance, car insurance, home insurance, life insurance, and a savings account. If anything goes wrong with me or my stuff, I know I'm taken care of. I have plans of protection, set up through the necessary systems, and paid for by myself. The great American capitalist economy is my green pasture.

But now that I've experienced this new understanding of the biblical image of green pastures, I have to wonder: *Have I lost sight of God a bit in the clutter of all my stuff? Do I really even need God on this journey?* I mean, according to my theology, Jesus is my boarding pass to the destination, and I already have that ticket in my pocket. So what need do I *really* have for him along the way? I pretty much have all the safeguards in place to enjoy my time here on earth.

Or do I?

Another day in the desert. Wylie E. Coyote halts to a stop. Like a choreographed dance move, we all simultaneously bob our heads forward. The bus doors swing open. "Come, let's go." The people in the front row of the bus aren't ready for the chase, and it irritates me because they're standing in the aisle, fidgeting with their fanny packs, in no hurry at all. Meanwhile, I can see well enough through the grimy windows, the only sign of our leader is a trail of footprints in the dust. Finally, the plug is pulled and the bus begins to drain itself of hikers.

Teachable moments permeate the walk. One just needs to pay attention and be a keen observer. To miss the journey—to set out only to see sites on the destinations—is to miss half of it, from my perspective. So myself and a couple other eager-to-learn students can always be found in a pack around our leader, devouring whatever bit of subsistence God gifts us through him. My pen works fast and furious so as not to forget a moment. It's a tricky act of coordination, exercising both my pen and my feet simultaneously on the jagged path. I keep thinking that a portable stenograph machine would be nice, except that I don't know how to use one. Maybe I'll hire a stenographer next time.

Our guide models the study tour after the concept of a rabbi leading his disciples. We can choose to benefit from the incarnate analogy or not. I'm loving it. I want to live it. This skeleton itself is a powerful reminder of discipleship, a thoughtful vehicle paired with the robust curriculum it delivers. As a tactile learner, it speaks as loudly to me as the verbal content of the faith lessons, conceivably even a decibel or two higher.

The relationship between a rabbi and his disciples is one of intensity. Our Bibles often translate the word *rabbi* as *teacher*, which only gets at a portion of its meaning. When I think of a teacher, I picture someone who stands before his students and relays information. Someone who delivers the data to the pupils, data that has at a prior time been delivered to the teacher by his teacher. All this in the hope that the said students will then give it back to him and receive a satisfactory grade. And the whole of this process, contained within the sterility of the classroom. Sometimes, when I think of a teacher, the image of spitballs spewing out from the mouths of disrespectful students and stifled giggles from the onlookers comes to mind as well, which only further illustrates the lack of respect today's students have for their teachers.

In Jesus' world, boys studied in the synagogue and by age twelve thoroughly memorized the entire Torah (the first five books of the Bible). And I thought it was insufferable to have to commit a few questions from the catechism to memory! But this was no punishing act for these young boys. Their passion about learning the Torah parallels American little boys today who fervidly play with LEGOs, climb trees, or triumph in the latest video game. After completing their initial studies around the age of 12 or 13, boys would go to various rabbis and ask them: "Can I follow you?" The rabbi would then ask a series of questions to determine whether or not the boy had perfected his memory work, had understood the teachings—if he had the potential to be a rabbi himself.

It was a privilege to be accepted by the rabbi, the highest calling for a young boy. Either the rabbi would say, "Come follow me." Or else he would say, "Go and learn the trade of your father," which was a nice way of saying, "Sorry, kiddo, you just don't make the cut. You were created for manual labor." Only the top grade-A students were privileged to follow a rabbi.

So it's interesting that Jesus gathers his disciples from where? Places such as the fishing boats and the local tax office. Jesus could have selected the best of the best students, the students who completed all the extra credit projects, elevating their grade A to an A-plus status. So why didn't he? Why did Jesus—God on earth—choose from among the worst of the students, the leftovers? Those whom the other rabbis had rejected and were already apprentices to their fathers? Shouldn't Jesus have the best? The whipped cream off the hot chocolate? The extra virgin olive oil?

But no, Jesus stirs up the system in a gesture that must have raised some eyebrows, crinkled some noses, shook some heads, set the gears of whispering gossip in motion. Instead of being approached by the students, *he* approaches *them* and says, "Come, follow me." It would have simply been unheard of! Jesus chooses the lowly boys, the ones last picked for the playground kickball teams. It is these ragamuffins he trusts to follow him, to transmit his way of living to the ends of the earth. Why does he do this? Is it possible that he was more concerned with a person's hands and feet than the information in one's head? Perhaps he wanted to train those whom he believed would most passionately walk the walk, rather than those who could smartly talk the talk. Perhaps.

This relationship between rabbi and disciple is one of incredible depth. Intensity. The students follow the rabbi for a few years. Leaving their families, they wander with him, as he not only teaches them what he knows but also shows them how to live. True disciples want to embody their rabbi. They want not only to follow his feet, but to actually be in his sandals. They want to be him. And eventually, they may go on to be a rabbi just like him for their own disciples.

This new understanding is profound. Can I really call myself a disciple of Christ, then? If Jesus walks up to me one day and says, "Come, follow me," would I do it? Would I actually drop my life plans and accept his plan for me? Would I be willing to step outside the American Dream and into his desert-bound footsteps? The question squanders away every moment of stillness. With this new knowledge of the weight of that word "disciple," I'm not sure I could. To be perfectly honest, I'm not even entirely sure I would want to. I mean, just turn your eyes upon Jesus. Look who he was, what he did, the things he said.

The rabbi Jesus, respected by multitudes, but hated by a profusion of others. Is that the life I want? I'm pretty sure I just want to lay low, to blend in, to nod and agree with those who've blazed a trail ahead of me, to avoid drawing attention to the swinging of my hatchet, a hatchet that might cut away from that well-worn path and set my feet moving in an unpopular, and possibly treacherous, direction. A path that could be lonely, that could be painful and difficult.

The rabbi Jesus, who went to the low places, sat with the wretched. Do I want to disburse my existence in the dank places, the premises devoid of light and purpose? Do I want to live in the corners that evoke fear and suicidal death wishes? I had in mind more of a cozy bungalow in a Thomas Kincaid painting with soft lights in the windows, giant honeysuckle twisted around a white picket fence, exhaling delicious sugared breaths, and a spectrum of colored hollyhocks forever in bloom perfuming the world with sweet fragrance. I mean really, what sort of nudnik would intentionally seek out the former?

The rabbi Jesus, who blatantly informed us that in turning away the hungry, the naked, the sick, we turn away him—a story I've heard many times, without ever really grasping it. I'm pretty secure in my Republican ideologies, and this seems contrary. I had understood that by ignoring the cries of the poor, hungry, and naked, we're actually somehow blessing them. The contradiction of Jesus' call to discipleship suddenly makes a mess of my intellectual faculties, getting them all tied up in knots as I try to process it.

The rabbi Jesus who went to hell and smashed the devil. Am I called to go to the hells of my world and pulverize the drudgeries of the evil one as well? I mean, for all intents and purposes, I'm certain I don't want to go near that one.

Or perhaps Jesus really is not my rabbi, as I have always assumed. After Jesus' resurrection in the Gospel of Matthew, he gives his disciples what is often referred to as the Great Commission. Jesus says, "Go therefore and make disciples of all nations, baptizing them in the name of the Father, the Son and the Holy Spirit." Notice to whom he says this: he says it to his disciples. So then, the Great Commission is about disciples making disciples.

Without understanding the relationship between rabbi and disciple, how can I presume to be carrying out the last will and testament of Jesus? Jesus, God in our midst. In my theological tradition, the emphasis falls on the baptizing portion of this commission. The primary focus is limited to telling a person who Jesus is and where he fits in God's plan of redemption. It can all be boiled down and explained over a cup of coffee, drawn out on a napkin. Just sign the dotted line and you have your ticket to heaven. It comes down to the destination and getting as many people *there* as possible.

As for the discipleship bit, I'm doing well if I avoid certain behaviors, such as sex outside of marriage, swearing, or voting for a Democrat. I've considered myself a prime disciple for most of my life, with the exception of a brief interlude in junior high when Christian music took a back seat to the bewitching, soothing, sultry love songs of Chicago on my cassette player, a time when I was more concerned with perfecting Michael Jackson's moon walk than Heidelberg Catechism Question and Answer One.

In its context, discipleship appears to be more about a proactive way of life, action beyond the churning of the gears in my head. If this plan of transmission from disciple to disciple trickles down flawlessly, then my life should mirror Jesus. The problem is, it doesn't. No doubt, there are occasional undertones of Jesus in the way I live. But if I'm honest with myself, I definitely can't be considered a true disciple of his.

Growing up at the edge of Lake Michigan, I became well acquainted with the thunderstorms that would gather over the lake and roll over us, releasing their heavy load. I was often caught out in the field, bent over some patch of asiatic lilies or on my hands and knees, wrestling the weeds among the rows of gladiolas when these storms welled up. Darkness would gather into a great wall and gradually crawl toward me, as if a thick heavy blanket were slowly being pulled over the earth, and I could sense the impending weight of it.

Now as I stand in the realization that I can hardly be considered a disciple of Jesus, a sadness swells over me and sweeps through me, much like one of these dark thunderclouds blowing in off the lake. It consumes the sun above and the earth beneath as it crawls forward and replaces the clear blues with dark hues of gray. It subdues me, humbles my spiritual narcissistic tendencies. I stand dumbfounded in the realization that I am not all I've always thought myself to be. Despite the great song and dance I continually work so hard to flawlessly put on, I'm not the super-Christian, mega-Jesus star I've always considered myself. The knees of my spiritual vanity begin to bend.

But as a lake-effect storm blows through, it clears the air, wrings out the insufferable humidity, and sharpens the senses. The world is left awash with a new freshness, a crisp clearness that hangs in the firmament above and drapes the earth beneath with intensified alertness. The greens are greener, the reds are redder, the blues bluer. And in the residual moments of being humbled and cracked in my grieved self-realization, a clarity begins to break in all around for me as well. My senses are sharpened and a new awareness settles over me.

This trip leads me to a crossroads, and I know I'll have a decision to make. His path or mine. If I choose discipleship, then I'm going to take it seriously. I don't jump into anything halfway. This is an all or nothing deal for me. Taking it seriously will require studying his life seriously. Here I am, claiming to base my whole life around this man Jesus, yet realizing that I really don't truly know him. Being aware of my lack of devotion to studying the text is an embarrassing self-admission. Can I live like Jesus if I really don't know him? But then if I do come to know him, will I really *want* to walk in those sandals?

As I've always understood it, faith is mainly a head thing, a deep knowing of the certainty of my particular theological understandings. This new comprehension of discipleship leaves the deep recesses of my mind and starts flirting with my heart, as if trying to figure out a new dance together. Before, they were somewhat swinging to the strum of their own guitars. Is faith supposed to be a thing on the move beyond the parameters of my head? Can it even be considered faith at all, if it *isn't* on the move?

That flow of life, which was supposed to be transferred from disciple to disciple, has clearly been disrupted over the course of the past 2,000 years. What am I to do about that? And to what extent had it been disrupted 500 years prior to now, when the theologies were written to which I so cling? The inner turmoil is private and becoming increasingly intense with each step in the dust of the rabbi. An introvert nail-biter, the white outer edges of my fingernails have entirely disappeared, and we're only one week into the trip.

Another day. We encounter a few ibex along the path. Ibex are a mammal similar in appearance to deer. The Bible sometimes refers to them as "ibex" and sometimes "deer." Regardless of what name you call it, it's truly an amazing creature to observe. We watch in bewilderment as they climb up cliff sides, scaling boulders the size of semi trucks. It's their feet we are so focused on. These hoofed extremities are astounding. They trek the cliffs as if they're the product of some sort of cross-breeding laboratory experiment. Perhaps a supernatural combination of Spiderman, a white-tailed deer, and a tree frog. I find myself holding my breath, thinking that with each step they are about to become venison burger.

"Don't ask for the easy path, but ask God for feet fit for the path." Our guide steers us to a different kind of prayer. *Feet for the path*, I think, while watching the ibex scale the mountain with ease. In my prayers, I've often asked God: "Give me an easy path, make everything all better. Kiss my injuries, bandage them up, and don't let it happen again. Please. In Jesus' name. Amen."

But now I'm sensing another new twist. Perhaps we ought not to pray for an effortless life, but for God to give us the feet we need to traverse the life he continually unfolds before us. This seems to make more sense with my new understanding of discipleship. Go to the places Jesus asks us to go, the places the Shepherd leads us. Trust Him to provide on that journey and pray for feet for that path. It's all coming together now.

But so much doubt grasps and claims all parts of me. Can I do this? Discipleship promises no easy path. I find myself in somewhat of a fixated trance, my mind swallowed up by these questions. I focus on the feet ahead of me—the feet of my rabbi on this expedition. This physical walk has become a litmus test of sorts for me. I remain one breathless step behind the rabbi for the duration of our time here. Where each of his feet pounds the ground, I place mine, so that there is only one set of tracks behind me after the dust settles. I grip the same edges of the same rocks as we climb mountains and navigate cliff sides.

As the hours wax and then wane under the heat of the Middle Eastern sun, I realize this has become a spiritual exercise for me, a symbolic picture of what I want my life to be like, should I decide to take that plunge into discipleship. A desire awakens within me, a desire to be so close to Jesus that for those who walk behind me there will be one set of footprints. I find myself wanting not only to walk his path but to be in his sandals, to physically be him to the world I encounter.

The decision finally comes on the banks of the Jordan River. The Israelites, terrified of water, saw it as the Abyss, the place where demons lived. One slip on a wet rock and they would be dragged away into this bottomless pit of torment forever. And so water was avoided at all costs.

I have a childhood memory of a thick panic pervading me, embezzling away my sense of security as I watched *The Wizard of Oz* on our black and white Zenith. Knowing I lived in an area where tornados occasionally touched down, sleep was unable to claim me for many nights throughout the season they were most likely to strike. I was terrified to the point where my blood ran colder than Christmas in Siberia. I would lay awake with my ears extra alert, keenly aware of even the sound of the slight whispers of each breath as it drew into my lungs and expired. Listening for that telltale rumbling train sound that precedes a strike, fear would not allow me to surrender to sleep. But this childhood anxiety of tornados pales in comparison to the ominous foreboding the Israelites had of water, the dreadful panic of being sucked away and swept down to the depths of the abyss.

When the Israelites headed to Jericho and happened upon this fast-moving river, what did God tell them to do? He told them to step off the bank into the rushing waters. He didn't say, "I'll part the water and then you can easily cross." He pronounced to them to step in *first* and *then* the water would part. Standing beside the bank with the water scrambling over and around the rocks, I can scarcely imagine what those poor Israelites must have been feeling. It would be like God asking me to walk into a level nine tornado. "Step into the infernal regions if I ask you to, and trust that I will make a way for you. Trust that I have a plan for you, that I will be with you."

In the past, if I had sensed God calling me to one thing or another and everything wasn't safely in place for that to happen, I would dismiss that voice. Surely, then, it wasn't the voice of God, couldn't be his will for my life. But now as I hear anew, God basically says, "If I say jump into chaos, you jump. Trust me. Follow me. I will give you feet for this journey. I will lead you to green pastures as necessary."

A poignant example from Jesus' life occurs right after his baptism. The gospels note that immediately following this dip in the Jordan River, Jesus "was led by the Spirit into the desert." The Holy Spirit leads Jesus into the desert, only to be tempted by Satan for forty days. If God can lead Jesus into a desert experience, what makes us think we should be exempt? Why do we pray so fervently to avoid such tumultuous times? If we truly are his disciples, if we truly are asked to walk in Jesus' footsteps, we should fully expect to be led occasionally into the desert.

So it boils down to this: my way or God's way. The information in my pot—what I learned about God growing up—doesn't give such an account of God's way for my life. This isn't necessarily a bad thing, but what I learned wasn't complete, and in some instances, the focus seems to have been a bit off, a tad skewed. Off just enough to significantly alter my faith walk. To this point, I had been more destination-focused than journey-focused, more head-focused than feet-focused. Through the experiences of these two galvanizing and illuminating weeks, I make my decision: I will hurl myself into the Jordan and fully submerge myself in God's plan. With that, I am baptized, dunked beneath the torrents of the Jordan.

Life breaks through the swirling surface, a new life with renewed focus on Jesus, beyond what he did for me. As a response to that deep, deep boundless love, I'll seek to know him—to know him intimately. And as I come to know him, I'll strive to live as he lived, to love as he loved. And so as I step, soaked and dripping, out of the Jordan onto the bank, I emerge a new creation—longing, aching to embody his essence.

The whole Israel experience shakes me out of my old reality. Many of my biblical images have been forever replaced. While the trip hasn't inexorably shaken the entire foundation of my theology, it has significantly altered my previously perceived ideas about faith and discipleship. Walking the land has given me a new passion for understanding the biblical text in its context, a previously foreign concept to me, but now so clearly and obviously important. I have a fresh fire inside me to live and breathe Jesus to the world.

My roots begin to push against the sides and bottom of my pot of certainties, hankering for expansion, for extension. The pressure of this growth creates a slight fracture in my pot of absolutes.

CHAPTER FIVE

Thwarted

AFTER TWO INTENSE WEEKS of study in Israel, El Al Air carries me home and I cross the threshold of the Longworth House Office Building as a new creation, redeemed and alive. Shockwaves still reverberate through my Dutch, Republican, Reformed self. There is no lack of bewilderment in realizing that we could have possibly gotten some things wrong. So if our biblical pictures are off, slightly skewed, then what else are we missing the Metro on? This is the question that begins to forever stick with me. Like a wad of gum inadvertently picked up off the sidewalk and fusing itself to the bottom of my Jackie O heels, I hear the soft sucking noise, feel a slight tug with every step I take. It becomes increasingly annoying and refuses to let go.

The obvious and inescapable transformation that I've walked away from Israel with is that if I'm going to call myself a disciple of Christ, I need to passionately strive to walk this earth as he did. And so I begin to ask myself what that looks like for me, in my place in this world. I've come back intensely excited, renewed in my faith, and determined to be yeast of the kingdom of God in the halls of government. Yes, yeast in the halls of government.

I collected various small rocks from places in Israel that deeply impacted my faith. Since everyone has to get to the congressman through me, I decide to prominently place the rocks on my desk on a rotating basis. A "Rock of the Week" sort of thing. If anyone asks, I can tell them the story of what God did and the specific ways of how my faith sprung to life in that place. Mini faith-lessons. One day some curious questioners walked in the door.

The congressman I work for occasionally has something on his schedule called "C Street." No one seems to know what that is, including the congressman's scheduler. There's great mystery surrounding the two men who come to the office during that time slot. Something about a congressional Bible study. The staff often speculates, though the congressman refuses to divulge specifics. But today, these two leaders of C Street have questions for me.

One pauses at my desk, picks up the rock of the week and turns it over in his well-manicured hands. "This is an interesting rock." He flashes the steely white teeth enfolded in his well-chiseled face. His eyes move from the rounded sloping form of the rock and scramble up me, landing on my face, "Can you tell me about it?"

I have an impelling testimony about the rock all rehearsed, but somehow the whole speech is lost on me, leaving my mind momentarily jumbled, yanking me off track. These men and their covert operations intimidate me. I inhale deeply. *Focus on the Shepherd. . . focus on his feet,* I silently remind myself.

"Well," I tuck a few renegade strands of hair behind my ear and clear my throat, "I've just returned from a couple amazing weeks studying in Israel. This is a rock from the Jordan River. Would you like me to tell you what God did there?"

The other equally well proportioned, easy-on-the-eyes man moves to my desk beside the other. "Please do," he says, dimples teasing me. "I'm intrigued."

I'm unsure if they are making a mockery of me but decide I will be strong and courageous. Unashamed of the gospel. Bold for the Lord.

I tell them all about the Jordan River and the chaos it represents. How God told the Israelites to head into that chaos, trusting him. I speak of my personal experience there, how I felt the power of God wash over and through me, bringing new life and new conviction to immerse myself fully into the chaos of this world, spreading *shalom* from within it.

They seem genuinely interested, so I continue with more historical, cultural, contextual details. The farther I take them into the narrative, the more personal I begin to get with the details of how this trip impacted my personal faith. Lost in the story, the elusiveness of these men fades and they become instead, simply two hungry souls. "And that is what God did at the Jordan River." I clasped my hands together on my desk, smiled and looked deeply into the walnut eyes of the two standing before me.

They stand silent for a moment. Seem spellbound.

One of the men's eyes seeks out the pile of rocks on a low shelf behind me. "Are those more rocks from your trip?"

I rotate my chair toward the small, disorganized heap. "They are."

"Do they all have such extraordinary testimonies?"

"They each have their own testimony, yes." I swivel back to them. "And each one folds into a part of God's larger story."

They briefly look at each other and then the quieter of the two turns back to me. "We'd really like to hear the stories of all your rocks, to learn more about your trip."

I'm stunned. This is unexpected. We set up a time to meet.

I really don't know much about these two guys, but they continually refer to their group of congressmen as "The Family." We end up meeting a few times in order for me to share as best as I can, the fullness of my experience in Israel. In time, they seem to gain more and more trust in me. My curiosity thickens one day when they invite me to help out with the 48th Annual National Prayer Breakfast.

Who are these guys? I keep wondering. *Shrouded in so much mystery. Organizers of the National Prayer Breakfast. Personal friends of many congressmen. Wanting to know every detail of my time in Israel. Something called C Street. Members of "The Family."* I rack my brain, unsuccessfully trying to pull all the fragments together. Perhaps I just need to trust them, as they seem to be more and more trusting of me. I accept their invitation to help out with the National Prayer Breakfast.

As the big day gets closer, I'm outright ebullient to be part of something spiritual on such a grand scale. My hopes soar for this gathering of presidents and other world leaders coming together to pray for spiritual guidance. Perhaps Bill and Hillary, seated at the head table, will be filled with the power of God and convert to the Republican Party. I can only hope and pray. The rest will be up to the Holy Spirit. Perhaps here, the yeast will work its way into the very heart of the D.C. dough.

Breakfast day. My eyes scan directly to the head table. There, I recognize evangelist Franklin Graham seated. And singer Amy Grant. And President Clinton and Hillary. Despite my Republican pride, it's amazing to be in the same room with the indisputably most symbolically powerful man in the world.

I remind myself I am here to serve food. The head server loads my arms and points me to a table directly in front of the President. Seated here is Kenneth Starr, the lawyer who led the charges against the President in the Monica Lewinsky scandal. I find it especially interesting that these two men are facing each other head on at a prayer event, where reconciliation seems to be the theme. Perhaps this is no coincidence.

As I turn in the direction of the table, my breath begins to quicken. Knowing I'll be standing a mere few feet from the President, my heartbeat accelerates with each step. Add to this, the worry over my inexperience as a waitress. A concern arises. At my ever-so-accelerating heart rate, I calculate that I'll be having a heart attack at approximately the time I reach the head table. I'll collapse and it'll be scrambled eggs and fresh fruit chunks all over Kenneth Starr's designer pinstripes, and Bill Clinton will have one more last laugh.

Terror raging beneath my exterior, I arm myself with an artificially constructed, peacefully pleasant facade. I move in close to my point of arrival. *Steady hands. Steady hands,* I keep telling myself. *Don't trip. Don't trip,* I remind myself. I'm sensitively aware of any possible destructive devises at my feet, staying clear of stray Gucci purse straps and extra lanky legs jutting out. I arrive at the table with the most pleasant smile possible. The thought comes briefly: *This is how it must feel to be in a Miss America contest—strutting and confident, but praying under my breath, 'Oh God help me!'*

I successfully distribute the food and am dutifully thanked. Unable to resist, I glance up at the head table. The President, with fork in hand, hesitates, and meets my eyes. I lift my chin a bit higher and smile. He gives pause to his fork midway, nods his head, and smiles back. I wasn't expecting this. Roses crawl up my cheeks. *He probably had a thing for Jackie O when he was a boy*, I decide. Still, I am eminently flattered and rather flustered that the President of the United States notices me. My feet seem stapled to the luxurious carpet of this great room. My legs won't budge. It feels like I've been standing here for ten minutes, though, in reality, it's probably been more like five seconds. *Focus on the Shepherd. Focus on his feet*, I remind myself.

Suddenly, I see photos of burned and chopped up babies in trashcans. Abortion. *This man wants to kill babies*, I tell myself, *an undercover agent of the devil.* And I recall the faces, the flesh and blood of homelessness. *This man wants to keep these people on the streets. He is determined to enable their desperation with his handouts, stealing from hard-working Americans—punishing those who work hard to earn their way in this world.* These powerful images free my feet from the floor. I head for the side wall, feeling the eyes of the President scrutinizing my backside. This is where I'm supposed to stand until summoned.

Fingers strumming her guitar, the smooth voice of Amy Grant runs over me like a bottle of just uncorked Merlot. While listening and waiting, my eyes eventually wander back to the President. I think to myself how strange a thing it is to see, in person, someone who seems so untouchable, so removed from, and above me. It's surreal. But really he's just another human being, no more special than me. He breathes from the same sort of lungs as I do, he chews his food and swallows it in the same order as most civilized people. He urinates and defecates on a daily basis, assuming his fiber intake is at a healthy level. He gets diarrhea after eating too much of a good thing. He probably wakes with sore muscles the morning after an extra strenuous run, same as me. He catches me looking his way and smiles. Embarrassed and once again blushing, I return a quick nod of benevolence and dart my eyes to the floor. *Dead babies and homeless humans*, I remind myself. *This man could be the devil in the flesh.*

In the days that follow, the two leaders of C Street want to hear more about my trip. As their excitement grows over my enthusiasm, we decide to work together to organize a congressional trip to Israel, led by the teacher with whom I had gone. The bread is being rolled and pushed on the kneading board, and I can almost smell the yeasty flesh of it baking in the oven. The three of us fly back to my congressman's district for a meeting at his house to plan the trip to Israel. Excitement fills the dining room table. Plans progress. I can't believe this is happening.

As I lie in bed that night, I imagine all these powerful individuals collapsing to their knees in surrender under the Middle Eastern sun. I see them washed in the Jordan, glazed and graced by the power of God swooshing over them. A great hope wells up within me—a hope that the larger corrupt government systems could change for good if God firmly grabs a hold of the hearts of these politicians. God is kneading a very plump lump of dough. Imagining the warm yeasty scent it will produce, I drift off easily into a sweet slumber.

After a few weeks, the trip leader calls to inform me that, after much prayer and consideration, he feels uneasy about leading the congressmen on this trip. His time, he suggests, is better spent teaching young people whose hearts and minds are still tender, pliable, and receptive to passionate teachings. He needs to pull out. It's a disappointing and premature punching down of the dough before it has had a chance to fully rise. The air is released, the swelling gone. With thwarted expectations, I decide God has something else in mind. Perhaps the yeast was meant to work its way through other means.

The next time the two leaders of C Street drop in, they invite me to a party at a house called "The Cedars." They've decided to demystify themselves a bit more to me, to let me take one more step into their world. Excited to find out more, I follow their directions to The Cedars on the following Friday night.

A lovely young woman greets me at the door, adorned with the same Miss America gleaming-bright-smile I had tried to emulate at the Prayer Breakfast. A funny feeling comes over me. My intuition screams at me, waving crimson flags. Something is a bit off here. Inside the lovely house, people mill about, and I'm introduced to a handful of astonishingly exquisite-looking young women. More strange feelings overwhelm me. I'm getting a *Stepford Wives* vibe from this place. They proceed to give me a tour of the house and then subtly pepper me with questions about how I came to know The Family.

In the shadow of a growing discomfort, I have a few questions of my own and politely ask: "What is this place? What is your purpose in being here?" Each woman responds exactly the same, in a rehearsed a tone, and much like a polished informercial sales pitch, "We are here to take care of the mansion." Big smiles.

I'm not sure I understand. "What mansion?"

"The mansion across the street."

More confusion. Take care of the mansion? I have a hard time imagining these women scrubbing toilets, waxing mahogany floorboards, spritzing chemicals, and wiping down windows. The Nancy Drew in me wants to know more. "Well who lives there?"

Two girls look at each other quizzically, and then a petite, brown-haired, fawny-eyed woman turns to me, "Politicians live there. World leaders stay there when they're in town. We serve them."

"Oh. Like, you do their laundry? Cook for them? Clean?"

"Well, whatever they need, you know? We are here to serve God by serving these men that he has placed in power—in whatever way they need."

"In *whatever* way they need" reverberates through my mind. Reading between the lines, I am stunned. I want to run from this place. So I do. I find an excuse to politely exit the premises. "We are here to serve God by serving these powerful men in *whatever* way they need." *Really? These are friends of The Family? How can this be? Have I been so naive? Did they invite me to the house to offer me a life of luxury in exchange for "taking care of the mansion?" In exchange for doing "whatever they need"?! What kind of woman are they mistaking me for?* My car drives home on the fumes of stupefaction, tainted with indignation that begins boiling over from within me.

I'm quick to inform the men of C Street, with a caustic-tainted tone in my voice, that the experience at the house was quite interesting. They sense me pulling away, sense my discomfort. Now that the Israel trip is off, they begin to lose interest in me as well.

My roommate is the Assistant Chief of Staff to Speaker Denny Hastert. There are positives and negatives to this arrangement. On the down side: She works until wee hours of the night and often sleeps on the office couch for several days in a row, so basically, I live alone. On the upside: She gives me access to various events, receptions, and people that I would not be able to experience without her.

One day the phone rings and it's her. The State of the Union address is at the end of the week. Each congressman gets one gallery ticket to the event to give away. Our office draws straws and a co-worker wins the ticket. But my roommate phones to say that her office has a ticket for me. As it turns out, the Speaker has an entire swath of tickets for his own special gallery booth.

"Well," she explains, "we've all seen it, heard it. Same thing every year, you know? We like to watch it on the TV in the office, give a running commentary, and have our own little party. You're invited to come to the party here afterwards as well. You can grab a beer, meet some of my coworkers, some more of the GOP congressmen. . ."

"Really? This is fantastic!"

"Yeah, it's a pretty neat experience to be in the room with the President, nearly the entire Congress, and the Supreme Court Justices. Just keep it on the low, okay?"

"I'm so excited! Thanks for thinking of me."

"No problem. I gotta' get back to work now." She hangs up.

Holy Smokes! Awesome! The trifecta in terms of government assemblies—all the checks and balances under the same roof—that happens but once a year.

Despite the knowledge that I will be going to hear President Clinton present as fact his exaggerated conclusions and dishonest projections, I'm extremely excited to be able to be in the company of the family and friends of the Speaker, as well as the rest of the faces of our government.

The days pass by slowly before the big night finally arrives. I stand in line at the second metal detecting checkpoint on the way to the gallery seating, ticket in hand. An extremely serious guard walks down the line verifying our tickets. "Ticket, ma'am?" he politely asks. I hand him my ticket. His face lights up, and he instructs me to follow him, bypassing the machine search for weapons. I'm important. My ticket confirms my importance. So important am I that I'm allowed entry with complete inside trust. It's a trust that says, "You are a friend of some very important people, and they trust their life in your hands. They trust that you will not walk in with a bomb strapped to your chest and blow them to pieces." I confidently breeze past everyone in line with my chin tilted a notch higher, knowing that they also now know that I am someone important. Surely they're all wondering who I am, even though I myself am somewhat unaware of why I'm being singled out.

He ushers me into what I assume is the Speaker's booth, in the back row aisle seat. Sitting next to me is a beautiful, middle-aged, African-American woman with wisdom wrapped around her eyes. An African-American Republican. *She found Jesus,* I think to myself. *How exciting.*

I'm feeling fairly giddy at being in this place on such a night. With an excitement that forgets my Jackie O. poise and bespeaks naivety, I ramble enthusiastically, gesturing to the woman next to me. "Can you believe we are in the presence of such distinguished people on such a momentous night? I mean, the Supreme Court Justices will be sitting right over there! The President, the most powerful man in the world will be sitting right there! All the members of Congress will be here standing and sitting and standing again, clapping then cheering then booing then clapping again! This has to be close to the most exciting night of my life! I've seen this on TV so many times and now I can't believe I'll be sitting in the actual room as it happens! I'm so excited! Isn't this just absolutely inspiring?" I'm downright giddy. She endears me with a sweet-as-punch smile, her eyes sparkling in such a way that tells me she knows something I do not, that this is old hat for her.

As we wait for the event to begin, I talk easily with this kind woman. She's a nice grandma type. If she were Dutch, she'd have a pocket full of Wilhemina Peppermints to pass down the row. I wonder who she is and how she got to be here. Before I get the chance to ask, in walks Jesse Jackson. He takes the seat in front of me. Perhaps he's mixed up, has come to the wrong booth. Surely this close friend of the President should be on the other side. "Oh my!" I think, "What a mix-up!" I grasp the arm of the kind woman and whisper with great expression, "*That* is Jesse Jackson sitting in front of us." She smiles, with laughter in her breath.

While we wait for the President to arrive, the three of us stand, stretch our legs, and talk. This is surreal. Am I standing here talking to Jesse Jackson like it's just another day? I glance down and see my congressman on the floor staring up at me with confusion registered on his face. I hadn't told anyone at the office I'd gotten this ticket. Seeing me talk to these Democrats, he probably wonders if I'm a spy, secretly working for the other side. Embarrassed, I quickly turn back to the conversation at hand, positioning myself in such a way that puts the frame of Jesse Jackson between us so the congressman's eyes don't meet mine again. *What is this prominent Democrat doing in the Speaker's booth anyways?* I wonder. Perhaps this also acts as the overflow booth for the President's section. He probably has so many friends that want to hear him on his annual big night, that he can't squeeze them all in his booth.

The woman next to me seems to have taken a liking to me. I certainly think she is a dear thing. She smiles with that twinkle in her eye. "So, will we see you at the White House party later?"

I stare at her dumbfounded. Speechless. Stop. Rewind. "What did you say?"

She smiles. "The White House party. You're coming, aren't you? We'll all be there. Maybe you'll meet the President." She winks.

Hollow and dumbly. "Oh. . . Um. . . Well, the thing is that I uh. . . I already. . . um, accepted an invitation to another party." Drat! A party at the White House? Now that would have been sensational!

Curiosity. "But how. . ." My question trails off as I realize that indeed there has been a mix-up with the tickets. MY ticket! Just then, in walks Chelsea Clinton with Mia Hamm, one of my worldly idols. Oh my. Could this night get any more exciting?

Everyone stands. The Supreme Court Justices enter. I refocus my attention, reaffix my feet to the floor and lift my hands up high, enthusiastically slapping them together for the Supreme Court. When they're all seated, I swing my arms down and *Whack!* I assume I've just smacked the guard in the groin and that he'll be doubled over in wincing pain. "Oh!" I immediately begin the spinal rotation to apologize. "I'm so sorry. . ." And then, ". . . Hillary." Face-to-face I am with the First Lady, whom I've just socked pretty solidly in the gut. A fine introduction this is.

But again, that familiar Miss America smile appears on her face. She continues on past as if nothing happened at all, gracefully descending the stairs, nodding her head politely at everyone in the gallery and at the millions of viewers at home, through the dozens of network cameras all focused on her.

While leaving the gallery after the speech, I turn to say goodbye to the kind woman. She is already walking down the hall in the opposite direction, clipboard in one hand, and her other arm protectively around First Lady Hillary Clinton. I shake my head and laugh under my breath. *Her assistant. The kind woman is an assistant to the First Lady of the United States of America.* Unreal. I have to admit, the evening is amazing, even if Bill Clinton, an agent of the devil, is at the head of it all.

My roommate clarifies something else for me. It turns out that if the President has extra tickets to the State of the Union, he gives them to the Speaker's office, and vice versa. I was given the President's extra ticket.

As I head out to my friend's party, my cell phone rings. It's my brother. "I swear I just saw you whack Hillary Clinton on TV! Way to go! She can consider that as being from all of us!" Good grief. Jackie O took a big back seat to blockhead Charlie Brown.

Sleep comes slow tonight. Events replay in my mind, and my thoughts trace back to the desert in Israel. I think on Jesus. Who he was, the things he did, the places his feet walked. *Am I on the wrong path again? Caught up in a state of giddiness over the powers of this world? Am I as excited to sit at the feet of Jesus as I was tonight to breathe the same air particles as some of the most powerful political forces in the world?* The answer is obvious and I feel ashamed. How quickly I've forgotten. How swiftly I've been seduced and lured away by the sultry smoothness of the indomitable.

God, forgive me.
Renew me.
Refocus me.
Give me eyes to see what you see.

Chapter Six

Growth Amid Thorns

Give me eyes to see. This becomes my prayer, my mantra.

Despite what I've been told time and time again, it now seems impossible to ignore the strong possibility that Jesus would be more of a grassroots guy. I find myself focusing more and more on the biblical text and the life of Jesus. With a renewed understanding of him, I have an increasingly difficult time wrapping my brain around the idea that if Jesus were living in Washington D.C. today, he would be working in a congressional office or residing at 1600 Pennsylvania Avenue, for that matter. Surely he would have sat on the throne of the Roman Empire if that were his intent. Most even expected him to come and reign from the high seat of the Empire, but instead, he chose instead to be among the people, to work from the bottom. Jesus was a grassroots guy.

Were he here today, then, wouldn't he be working directly with these people of the streets rather than commanding the largest army in the world? And, after all, didn't he say, "Whatever you do to the least of these, you do to me. Whatever you do not do for them, you do not do for me?" This line of thought leads me to wonder: *What if Jesus isn't just helping them, but is, in fact, one of them?*

It's impossible to ignore. The notion plagues me. For days it consumes me, devours every other thought about any other thing that enters my mind, while exponentially increasing its territory to the far corners of my brain. Tossing and turning and getting all twisted up in my sheets at night, I do everything short of counting sheep to try to still my mind. I keep seeing the scene over and over. Jackie O, righteous head held high, turning her heels on the relentless beggars, all in the name of Jesus and his Republican footmen. I turn it all over and around in the complex places between my ears. The neurons relentlessly fire away. World War III completely contained within my skull.

Back and forth like a fierce match of tug-of-war, one minute I'm certain that I should be bringing *shalom* to the chaos of these streets in a very practical, tactile way as Jesus did. But then the very next minute, I'm back attempting to find rest in the certainty of my lifelong convictions: "Jesus, the Son of God, second person of the Trinity, born of the virgin Mary, suffered under Pontius Pilate, voted for George Bush, was crucified, died, and was buried. Three days later, he rose again from the dead so that a Capitalist economy could rise to the occasion of getting me lots of stuff in this life, until Jesus sweeps in to take care of me in the life to come. And Lo, the poor will always be with you, so don't waste your precious time and financial resources." That's all in the Bible somewhere, isn't it?

And I'm certain I recall something somewhere from the apostle Paul (or was it John Calvin?) that states laziness causes homelessness, and handouts only encourage that laziness and therefore perpetuate the cycle of homelessness, thereby strongly suggesting that we avoid giving handouts. These are the indisputable facts. Certainly the entire community of believers that surrounded me and nurtured my faith and understanding of all things couldn't be wrong, could they?

I have to admit that I've definitely spent more quiet time in my life with Rush Limbaugh than I have with Jesus. I was no exception in my home community where people tune in to conservative talk radio religiously. Is it possible these voices led me astray, led an entire community astray? Had they blazed for us a new path of *self*-righteousness? Had we fine-tuned our ears to the voices of men like this, and by faith followed their words rather than the words of the Good Shepherd, while subtly distorting Jesus' message, bit by bit? Had their voices gotten indistinguishably intertwined with the voice of Jesus? If so, how can I disentangle the chords of truth from the strands of refuse?

In the ethical treatise, *On Virtues and Vices*, the author, usually attributed to Aristotle, speaks of *phronesis*, which means "wisdom to take counsel, to judge the goods and evils and all the things in life that are desirable and to be avoided, to use all the available goods finely, to behave rightly in society, to observe due occasions, to employ both speech and action with sagacity, to have expert knowledge of all things that are useful." In plain English, *phronesis* involves looking at the context of a situation and determining the best action, in that given circumstance.

The Republicans may have gotten a broad concept right: Federal Government has gotten too big for its britches—a realization of the very thing the founding fathers warned about. How can we expect Big Government to speak effectively for and come to the aid of its citizens when it has gotten so big and our representatives so far removed from the very citizens they seek to represent? Big Government seems incapable of effectively applying *phronesis* to deal effectively and efficiently with issues like poverty. In fact, as the population of the United States multiplies and diversifies, it seems absurd to expect the Federal Government to be able to connect to its variety of subcultured citizens. Not to mention, our representatives are, in reality, no representation at all of these various subcultures, but rather products of the most wealthy and privileged class. This privileged life further renders the decision-makers incapable of understanding the needs of their average and less-than-average constituents. So if the national government is somewhat ineffective, can we depend on the citizens with cash in their pockets to voluntarily lend a hand to those in need within their local communities?

Well, I don't have to look far to see. Despite the swift flow of abundant cash in this great city, poverty continues to cling to its streets, warming itself by the sewer grates, scouring the trashcans for sustenance. From what I can tell, cash in the pockets largely stays in the pockets. Despite the claim that if we have lower tax rates we'll have more money to give to the poor, evidence points to the contrary, so I'm skeptical about buying into that argument.

Do the Republicans tend to promote policies that favor the wealthy and lead to a further widening of the gap between the rich and the poor, thereby creating the very systems that lead to disparity in the first place? I'd like to believe they aren't intentionally creating this disparity, but in the least, is it possible that they are guilty of ignoring the ways in which poverty is affected by the policies they promote? Do they altogether avoid asking the question of how their policies affect the poor? And when a particular piece of legislation proves detrimental to the least among us, do they simply ignore its outcome on that class of people?

I'm reminded of these words from Sir Thomas More in his work, *Utopia*: "For if you suffer your people to be ill-educated, and their manners to be corrupted from their infancy, and then punish them for those crimes to which their first education disposed them, what else is to be concluded from this, but that you first make thieves and then punish them?"

The system often creates the very problems it later shakes its fist at. So what is the answer? What is the most viable solution? Shouldn't we seek out and attack the causes of this cancer rather than continue to spend so much research, time, and money on simply treating the symptoms of the wounds that fester?

My mind never shuts down. Tylenol PM doesn't work. Even Enya is powerless to lull me to sleep. I am Jacob, and God is in a wrestling match with me. I half expect to get out of bed each morning with a lame hip and a new name.

Then one day as I'm on my way to work, the answer comes to me as clear as a Capitol Hill shoeshine. In a moment of hushed quiet on the packed 8 AM Metro, that still small voice comes to me, in a not-so-still, not-so-soft way. It is barely above a whisper, and at the same time it is a roar. It is not the voice of God, and yet it is. It's the unmistakable voice of my former teacher, mentor, and Israel trip guide pacing to and fro, slamming his hat into the dust, frustrated over his clueless disciples. "You want to call yourself a disciple of Jesus? Then you better be living as he did! You better be walking as he walked!"

Perhaps Jesus isn't a Republican after all, or a Democrat, for that matter. Perhaps. Perhaps he's simply a man on the move, bringing *shalom* to the places of chaos from *within* the chaos, rather than from outside of and above it. Perhaps it's time for me to get off my ergonomic swivel chair and at least do some small part. This nagging suspicion births my top secret plan: Grassroots Jesus. It's time to get a grip on what really matters. I take a hard look at my reflection in the window of the Metro as it approaches Union Station. I see beyond the fitted suit, past the Jackie O hairstyle, deeper than the perfectly painted face, and I examine the core of me. "Good grief. Look at you." My head shakes from side to side.

The Grassroots Jesus Plan goes something like this: Twice a week I trek from the Union Station Metro stop to the Capitol, and back again in the evening. After work, I plan to invite an individual living on the streets to eat a meal with me in the food court at Union Station. I'm not so naive as to give cash handouts, knowing there's a good chance it will go straight to the liquor store. No doubt that's what I'd do if I were in their depressing shoes. So I opt for a hot meal and conversation, if the individual so desires.

Give me eyes to see.

The plan works fairly well at first. I'm privy to personal stories, some that squeeze my heart and pain me in places of which I was completely unaware, and others that simply indulge me with memories of better days. Some are incapable of common social interactions. Many take the food and walk away without a word. One elderly woman, with gray oyster eyes, giggles all the time. Like a schoolgirl, she giggles and constantly smiles but never speaks a word at all, seemingly oblivious to the suffering around her, perhaps even her own. Some thank me, others never do. But mostly it's just good to come to see and appreciate these "lazy bastards" as fellow human beings—created and loved by God—walking the same broken planet as me, and to treat them as such. Is this *phronesis* in action?

In the case of my homeless friends, it's easy for many of us who are middle and upper class Americans—coming from safe and comfortable backgrounds—to judge them as being homeless due to laziness because, in our own existence, it's an unimaginable lifestyle. Given the advantages I've had and the booming economy, were I living like this, it probably would be my own fault. But when you apply phronesis, in an attempt to understand all the processes and influences that have brought an individual to the point of homelessness, any human with any amount of empathy should understand that, with few exceptions, they are not simple laying on park benches because they are lazy. The string of events that parked them on the bench is far more nuanced and complicated than that.

The Grassroots Jesus Plan starts getting a little expensive for my meager government paycheck, as I barely make enough to go out to eat twice a week on my own, let alone to treat someone else. So I come up with Grassroots Jesus Plan B, which is to fill my briefcase with PB & J's and pass them out. This seems the most efficient possibility, though I do lament the fact that I won't have as much opportunity to hear the individual stories and build relationships. On the upside, I begin to have my "regulars," and that's nice because I'm soon able to attach some names to faces, and eventually those faces begin to smile upon my approach. And I find myself smiling back and thinking, *Jesus.* And then one day, I have a revelation of sorts: Perhaps the yeast I so long to be and to disperse is subtly enfolded in the air pockets of the bread of these peanut butter and jelly sandwiches.

~ ~ ~

One chilly evening in early April, I head out to dinner with a handsome, strawberry blonde-haired gentleman who happens to work in the Clinton Administration. He takes me to an exquisite black-tie restaurant. I relish any opportunity to wear my classy black Audrey Hepburn dress (think *Breakfast at Tiffany's*) that I save for just such occasions. I adorn my neck with a strand of pearls and clasp my ears with matching earrings.

William, a perfect gentleman, holds the door open for me, slips my coat down my shoulders, and slides out my chair at the posh restaurant. I look at my menu with thick, gold-embossed premium prices, enticing us to dine in courses, each with its own premium price. My plate arrives with a miniature-sized meal, arranged with such beauty, such artistic splendor that I find myself holding my breath each time my fork hesitantly displaces a vegetable. A bottle of Cabernet slides down easily between the two of us, and conversation is just as easy—in fact, seems to be getting easier as the bottle slowly empties. I discover that William is a Christian, pro-life Democrat, and somehow this sits pretty well with me. He speaks eloquently of his concern for the marginalized and defenseless in society. He is passionate about caring for and restoring life to both the unborn and those suffering under conditions of poverty and discrimination. This is the first truly consistent pro-life person I've met in Washington, where most people seem completely loyal to whatever positions fall within their party lines.

With plenty of stomach space left for dessert, we each order our own. Like the meal, my dessert is absolutely lovely—a monster-sized white plate with a rich chocolaty lump of something or other, barely bigger than a quarter, placed directly in the center, with raspberry sauce thoughtfully drizzled all over the plate and crystallized, edible pansies cloistered in small clumps around the edges.

Afterwards, we decide on a stroll down the sidewalk under the half moon to walk off the wine. As we turn a corner, we nearly stumble on a man keeled over on the sidewalk, his face in a puddle of vomit, empty vodka bottle tipped over beside him.

Give me eyes to see.

Unaware that I have stopped, William instinctively steps around him and continues walking and talking, as if we have not just stepped past a human being lying in his own vomit.

I know this man. It's Jack, a Vietnam veteran. He's one of my fairly regular sandwich recipients. I try to turn him over a bit, to shake him awake. William realizes what I'm doing and turns back, horrified. "Christy, what are you doing? He's filthy! You'll get vomit all over your dress! He could be dangerous. Step away before you get hurt!"

I'm matter of fact. "William, he needs help. Look at him."

William shakes his head, remains unmoved, and says under his breath, "God! I'm so sick of these bastards pissing and puking all over our sidewalks! Disgusting!"

I shoot him a look of disappointment. I'm burning with a frustrating rage inside. *What the hell was all that eloquent talk about back in the restaurant? Caring for the poor, my ass! Huh! Sure, he's concerned for the poor as long as he doesn't have to get his hands dirty! A fine politician he'll be someday!*

Just then, a swooning young couple holding hands stops beside me. The man sports faded, ripped jeans with an assortment of chains hanging off the pockets of his faux leather jacket. A roughly stitched-on skull patch hangs precariously in place on the back of his jacket. Matted hair styled with a sticky-looking, greasy substance overshadows his face, and tattoos girdle his fingers. "Whoa. Do you need some help here?" he asks.

"Yes, please." I point to a drugstore across the street. "Can you run over there and get some paper towels and a bottle of water?" I quickly pull a five-dollar bill out of my coat pocket and hand it to him.

"No dude, it's okay. I got it." He pushes my hand and my money away and proceeds to cross the street.

His girlfriend doesn't hesitate to bend down and help me. I notice her crow-black hair with red streaks and blond roots pushing through. She annoyingly smacks her gum, which must have been days old because her breath reeks of rot-mouth and seems to take direct aim at my nostrils from between her missing front teeth. A swastika necklace drapes her neck amid swirling tattoos of thorny roses that crawl up her neck from behind the folds of her oversized black hoodie sweatshirt and curl up around her ears. *An unlikely helpmate,* I find myself thinking.

"His name is Jack," I tell her. "He's a Vietnam veteran. He attempts to numb the memories away whenever he can afford to. Guess I don't really blame him. Can you help me drag him away from this filth?"

"Yeah, of course." She doesn't hesitate. As we slide him away from the center of the walkway and against the brick wall of the building, her boyfriend returns and hands me a plastic bag.

Jack groans, swinging his arms clumsily at nothing in particular. "Thanks," I say, reaching for the paper towels.

Willing myself not to gag, I wipe down Jack's face and wipe off his own vomit from the front of his shirt. "Jack." I soft-slapped his face to bring him to alertness. He cracks his lids apart slightly. "Jack. I have some water. You need to drink some water." Unscrewing the lid, I put the bottle to his lips. He takes a little in and chokes it down.

As if time suspended itself, I finally recall that I'm on a date. Disappointment, disgust, and disinterest wash over me as I look up. There, William stands aloof, at a distance with his arms folded. "Thanks for dinner, William. You should go now. I can find my way to the Metro. I might be here a little while."

William hesitates for a moment, shakes his head, opens his mouth to speak, but instead turns and walks away. The young couple offers to sit with me. "Thanks, guys," I say quietly to them, humbled by their kindness. We all sit quietly around Jack, whispering gentle words of encouragement, slowly pouring small sips of water between his crusty lips. Jack empties about half the bottled water and suddenly becomes tired. He mutters something incoherent and lies down to sleep. I prop the remainder of the paper towel roll under his head. *Probably the closest thing he's experienced to a pillow in a long time*, I think to myself.

Leaving the water bottle beside him, I again thank the young couple for their help. In a gesture of selfless love and kindness, the young man removes his worn jacket and drapes it over Jack, who would certainly be waking to cold and shivers were it not for the extra layer. When the young man removes his coat and rolls up the sleeves of his well-worn Guns & Roses t-shirt, drug-contaminated, gnarled veins reveal a plethora of infected points of needle entry on his bare arms. My breath catches in my throat as the two lovers stand up, swivel around, clasp hands, and head off down the sidewalk. I, too, stand and head for home. "Sleep well, Jack."

On my way to the Metro, I realize that I never got the names of the couple that helped me out, but I am certain that God will never forget them.

Suddenly, a new stench sickens me as I ride the Metro that glides ever so smoothly down the tracks. It's the stench of disappointment, the smell of an unfortunate revelation. Turns out that William embodies no more than a suave, disingenuous political rhetoric. I can't help feeling a bit angry by his charade. I thought I'd discovered a rare person truly concerned with the sanctity of life, not exclusively from conception to birth but beyond that. Over Merlot and fine china, William duped me into believing his concern for the marginalized people in society—the hungry, the homeless, the destitute. Yet, in the heat of the street, William would not place his hands nor walk his feet in the devastating places. The veneer of his empty rhetoric seems worse than anything I had witnessed that night.

I continue with my Grassroots Jesus Plan B through the spring. During this time, I persistently and inwardly tread questions regarding the Republican agenda but am somehow able to compartmentalize the work I do in the office from the work I'm doing in the streets. That is, until one damp spring day.

Avoiding the outside drizzle, I walk swiftly in the underground corridor between the Longworth House Office Building and the Capitol, when my friend Michael—presumably the most dogmatic Republican staff member on the Hill, motor mouth, and first class political nerd—closes in on me after I pass through the metal detectors beneath the Capitol.

He's all worked up, informing me that my secret cover has been blown. I've been caught handing out sandwiches. He begins chastising me, calling my actions a betrayal of the Republican principles, which I am unofficially sworn to uphold. I smile, thinking he's being sarcastic. But this response only further annoys him as he continues to tell me that I'm being thoroughly naive in thinking that handing out sandwiches is doing anything but hurting the homeless in the long haul.

I can't believe he's being serious. He then proceeds to have the gall to inform me that any one of the people on the street can be in a congressional chair if they want to be. "They just have to get off their lazy asses and clean up a bit."

"And by the way," he adds, as the other Republican robots had, "the things you're doing in your congressional office, the policies your congressman supports—these are the real, true and lasting things that help them."

Shocked at the anger in his voice, that he seems somehow threatened by Jackie O on the loose in the streets of D.C. with a briefcase full of PB& J's, I stop beside the corridor wall of displayed winning entries in the Congressional High School Art Competition and swing around to eye him straight on. I tend to be a person of few words, slightly more an introvert than an extrovert according to the Myers-Briggs personality assessment. Always thinking about things deeply, but usually so much so that by the time I have reached any sort of conclusion, the conversation is onto something else, and the opportunity to speak is lost. Today isn't that kind of day. I have been quiet long enough.

"Horse shit!" I clear my throat and gather my thoughts for not quite a full second. "How many of these homeless people have you talked to? How many of their stories have you heard? You are a world away from the deep-seated horrors they have lived through: The Vietnam vets hurled into hell by their government and survived just enough intact to drink the memories away! Others having endured terrible abuses the likes of which you cannot even begin to fathom! And others with severe mental illness and nowhere to turn for help or medication! You will not even be able to find it in the distant places of your imagination to begin to comprehend the lives these people have lived!"

I closed the space between us, as representatives rushed through the tunnels to cast their vote in the House chamber. I was almost close enough now for him to feel my breath on his face as I began spewing out my frustration over his unsympathetic ignorance: "Most congressmen were raised in loving families and had the privilege of a strong education, and you can't underestimate the power of that. Even if the actual physical potential is somewhere within the street people to be members of Congress, for many of them, their emotional and psychological state has been so completely devastated that the possibility of it isn't even within the grasp of their dreams! And let's not forget that it takes millions of dollars to win an election in this country! So don't tell me that any of these people who spend their days lying in the filth of the streets could simply take a shower and win a congressional race! You, my friend, are the naive one!" I turn my back on my disbelieving, huffing friend and proceed down the corridor, feeling like a lion and yet like a lamb.

Late that night, as the moon rises and takes its course, I lie awake once again, reflecting on the encounter, knowing I'm in for another one of those sleepless nights. I remind myself that my friend is pretty extreme in his Republican positions, that most Republicans wouldn't make such ridiculous accusations. Many would even applaud my efforts, given that I'm helping people out at my own expense rather than at the government's expense. But for me, the encounter spotlights the general Republican attitude that the poor are poor simply because they are lazy, and that the government has no business taking money from hard-working Americans and using it to enable the poor with handouts.

Most Americans would insist that if they could keep their own money in their own hands, then they would have more money available to contribute more effectively to various charities and non-profit organizations. But if helping the underprivileged is supposed to be a non-government choice and responsibility, then I have to wonder why, in cities like this, overflowing with cash, so many destitute people dot the streets in desperation. Clearly, not much of the personal wealth meets the streets. This dramatic gap between the rich and poor that I witness daily testifies to me that when left to the individual, the job will probably not get done. It seems to me that when we have more cash in our pockets, rather than giving more to the poor, we—myself included—typically increase our mortgage, add a new car payment, or take an exotic vacation, before we give to the least of these.

But when it comes down to it, isn't our nation basically a large community? Shouldn't we *want* to help each other out? Shouldn't we feel privileged to lend a hand, to turn in a portion of our earnings, if it means our brother, fellow citizen, and human being created and loved by God will have the basic necessities in life? In this nation of individualism, we seem to have forgotten this idea of community. Our individualistic, selfish ambitions compete for the latest, the biggest, and the best. "More for me! More for me! More for me! More of what moth and rust destroy at the expense of basic needs for those who happen to be birthed into less fortunate circumstances. As for those filthy street people, they can fend for themselves. Charity only produces dependence on more charity." We easily embrace the legal notion of "innocent until proven guilty." Can we turn this principle of legal justice into a principle of social justice?

Right-wing Christians often seem to be the staunchest supporters of individualism, on the front lines of demanding lower taxes. We want more for ourselves. We don't want the systems of government to care for those in dire situations because they get what they deserve and we, by the same rights, deserve what we worked so hard for.

But when I think of the Jesus I encountered in Israel, caring for the least of those among us is so obviously central to embodying the Kingdom of God. The early Christians shared everything—everything. They turned in all of their cash and possessions, a 100% tax rate so that no one would be in need. And they apparently did this willingly, non-begrudgingly, even happily. Having witnessed the deep peace and contentment that comes from a life of simplicity and deep authentic community, people ran to be part of it, chose willingly to give up all their individual possessions. They eagerly embraced those in the gutters and willingly sacrificed their individual rights for the larger benefit of the community, a community of people created and loved by God. The spirit of the followers of Jesus is one of an impossible love for those living in the margins.

I begin feeling tremendous anxiety over what I was taught growing up. This marriage between Christianity and the Republican Party no longer seems God-ordained. How did I never see this before? Is there something inherently wrong with the theology that has been worked into the soil of my pot? Something that has led generations of Christians to embrace this political attitude that focuses so heavily on *me* and *preserving my individually hard-earned stuff*?

And what of that still small voice—that still small voice of Jesus? "Whatever you do for the least of these you do for me. Whatever you do not do for them you do not do for me." There's not much room for voices like that in a country that prides itself on independence, wealth, power, and extravagance, all via the vehicle of selfish ambition. It appears that our right-wing political attitudes of individualism have bled into the attitudes of our faith.

Now, I see quite plainly. The fundamental Republican attitude of fighting to protect me-and-my-hard-earned-stuff was not the attitude of Jesus. In fact, it seems in direct opposition to the way of Jesus.

If Jesus were here today, he would not be a Republican. But when I think of Jesus and the sort of community he put forth, a scary political word does enter my mind: "Socialism." Would Jesus be a socialist? Socialism is one of the most feared words in the vocabulary of a right-wing Christian. It invokes images of the devil and his dark angels. And yet so much in the way Jesus talked and walked smells of socialism.

I begin to panic at the thoughts I've allowed to enter my mind. Perhaps the devil *has* taken up residence in my head, has sunk his claws, torn through all my layers of skin, whispering lies and deceit to me, convoluting my thoughts. I whittle away the hours of moonlight, wrestling with the devil. Or is it God who tackles me? I'm not really sure.

Over the next few weeks, I begin to slowly question and dissect the Republican agenda as a means to understand it and hopefully find some measure of justification in it. The thing that stops me in my tracks is the single issue that looms large over the heads of all Christian Right-wingers: abortion. Come election time, that word is dangled before us in every way, from gruesome photos on billboards to Sunday morning sermons. If Democrats are capable of inflicting pain on innocent babies, shredding their little bodies until the heart beats no more, then they are capable of all things evil. Life is precious. Is this issue alone enough to continue fueling my engine to shout for the Republican agenda?

Life is precious. Yes. Life is precious.

But as I objectively pick this issue apart, even the pro-life movement has some serious snags. Right-wingers insist that a pregnant woman must have her baby. Yet, they also insist that our taxes not be wasted on healthcare programs that provide affordable or free healthcare for herself and that baby. How can the woman afford prenatal care or postnatal care, or regular health checkups for the baby? We also don't want to spend more taxes to ensure that the woman receives a strong education in the first place—the evidence is strong that better education for women directly correlates to fewer unwanted pregnancies. And when this baby is born, we don't want to offer the mother job training and a career with full benefits that pays enough for her to afford child-care, in addition to the general cost of living. The child is then born into a life of poverty, which often results in a life of crime. These women and their babies are set up to fail. And so "the sanctity of life" is not really what it claims to be, but rather it overflows with the poison of hypocrisy.

Further, it becomes more and more clear, as I witness behind-the-scenes political machinations, that Republican lawmakers actually have little motivation to overturn Roe v. Wade. They would lose their single greatest issue motivating the Religious Right to cast a vote their way each election cycle. People are coerced into being single-issue voters—*it's the Christian thing to do*—when the realities facing our nation are far more complex. "Vote for me, I'm pro-life" hangs like a carrot forever dangled in front of the faithful, coaxing them to continue marching to the Republican beat.

If we are going to insist that pregnant girls and women have their babies, then we must also insist on providing for them in that event. If we insist on not paying the taxes to fund such programs, then as followers of Jesus, we better be willing to take her into our home, pay her medical bills, model basic life skills, and help her further her education so she can put food on the table and a roof over her baby's head. The early Christians would have done so immediately and without question. Community is community. These initial Christian communities emptied themselves in order to serve the least of those in their society. When one suffered, everyone suffered. This was the body of Christ. This was the attitude of Christ. And this ought to be the attitude of his disciples today—Republican, Democrat, and otherwise.

What about the Democrats, then? Is a strong central government that can care for all our needs the answer? In general, their policies and rhetoric seems more sympathetic to the needs of the multitudes of destitute people. Their call for those who spend weekends floating on their yachts to stop benefiting from so many tax loopholes, while others struggle at three jobs just to pay their medical bills or put food on the table, seems reasonable enough. But on the other hand, it also seems that we daily uncover more and more instances of waste, fraud, and abuse in our Federal Government programs. So many millions of dollars go disappearing with no paper trails—lost in a complicated mess of bureaucracy.

Beyond the waste, fraud, and abuse, I have to wonder if a centralized Federal Government is actually *capable* of being in touch with the reality of the daily grind of its citizens, when it is so far removed from those citizens. Not only is the government disconnected from its citizens as a whole, but the individual representatives, living in their posh surroundings, dining with millionaires and top business persons from around the world, are equally removed from the daily lives of their constituents. Perhaps they should be required to regularly dine with their constituents who sit on the bottom rung of the socio-economic ladder rather than those who sit on the top. If a politician would cross the tracks in order to share a meal, talk face-to-face, feel the breath and very heart of a poor man beating beside him, if a friendship could be forged between these two, it may go a long way in promoting mutual respect and effecting policy. But this idea seems closer to a Hallmark movie than to reality.

I find no easy answers, no simple political solutions. Gone are those simplified days of my childhood when all the answers were so easy and obvious. Fractured sleep becomes normal sleep for me. Long lost are the moments when sweet dreams and lullabies whispered to me throughout the night.

The only concrete conclusion I'm able to arrive at is that I cannot jump fully on board with either the Republican agenda or the Democrat agenda. Republicans put policies in place that often create poverty and many issues that stem from it, while Democrats promote sometimes ineffective, out-of-touch-with-reality policies to deal with those issues. And then there is a larger issue that spans and corrupts both parties, an issue which seems to be worsening as the years go by—so many spineless politicians (of both parties) dismissing their constituents and pampering the large corporations in order to maintain their own positions of power. This broader problem leads to both parties creating the disparities that further widen the gap between the rich and the poor, spawning even further socio-economic problems, as well as bringing about the promotion of ineffective policies to deal with those disparities. This umbrella of widespread corruption in the halls of our government all around magnifies the predicament of the citizens it is supposed to protect.

A working political answer might be to significantly decentralize the Federal Government on one critical condition: that communities of Christians actually take the biblical text—and Jesus—seriously.

In Micah and other Old Testament prophetic books, the authors advocate principles that today we might identify as being socialist or progressive. These ancient authors gave sharp warnings against the rich taking advantage of the poor and stockpiling riches for themselves at the expense of others. In a fallen world full of self-interested people, the tendency within societies is for wealth to be unevenly distributed, for the vast majority of money and power to be in the hands of a very few. This doesn't sit well with God. In the book of Leviticus, God sets up an economic system that promotes equal distribution. Every fifty years, God calls his people to celebrate the Year of Jubilee. During this year, all slaves are freed, all debts are cancelled, and all land—which was once equally divided among the people—is given back to the family to whom it was first given. All economic disparities are leveled. Every fifty years, when material realities increase unequally among the people, the playing field is leveled. This regular checking and balancing prevents disparities from ever getting too out of hand.

When Jesus came around, he too speaks more about loving our neighbor than anything else, though this is definitely apart from government: "Give to Caesar what is Caesar's, and to God what is God's." Jesus spent time with those on the ground, with the least of those in that society, those on the edges. He was not working from within the government, though he was not afraid to harshly criticize various injustices carried out on behalf of the government. He was himself often dependent on handouts as he sat with and among society's filth. Certainly, if he had intended to work from the top down, as many expected the Messiah to do, he would have done it. But he flipped that expectation on its head. So, as his disciples, ought we to be with and among society's filth as well?

In the first century, the Roman law required Jews to carry the pack of a Roman soldier for a mile, if requested. These very soldiers enforced the Roman law, marching with weapons drawn, demanding that the ever-increasing taxes be paid. Instead of rising up against these soldiers, demanding that taxes be lowered, Jesus tells his followers to carry their pack for two miles instead of one.

Again, the early Christians seemed to have a good grasp on Jesus' vision of what Christian community entailed. They shared and had everything in common. Listen to the observations of the Roman Emperor Julian, despite his rejection of Christianity: "Atheism [referring to Christianity] has been specially advanced through the loving service rendered to strangers, and through their care for the burial of the dead. It is a scandal that there is not a single Jew who is a beggar, and that the godless Galileans [Christ-followers] care not only for their own poor but for ours as well; while those who belong to us look in vain for the help that we should render them." It seems that even in ancient Rome, the government could not, or did not, effectively care for the destitute in the way the local Christian communities could and did, with their somewhat socialist philosophies.

Have we drifted so far from the center of Christianity, become so seduced by the promises of finding fulfillment in the lifestyles of individualistic capitalism that we are incapable of returning to a place of humbly embodying the essence of Jesus? Is it too late to expect followers of Jesus to give up this deeply embedded individualism in order to embody the selfless essence of Jesus? If we push for a decentralized national government, where the power shifts to the local communities, will Christians actually step up to the plate? It would be mandatory for us to do so. Some of Jesus' most harsh words are for those who claim to know him yet turn a deaf ear to those who cry out from the gutters.

Are we willing to take the homeless under our roofs, or would we be too concerned about someone wrecking our hard-earned stuff? Are we willing to open our homes at mealtime and bedtime for those whose stomachs rumble and who have no place to rest their head? Might we actually be willing to do that? Can we settle for humble dwellings in order to have more financial resources at our disposal to give to those who have nothing? Are we willing to *truly share everything* with *anyone* in need?

Jesus went all the way to the cross and instructed his followers to take up their crosses as well. A successful decentralized government would seem to hang on that one precarious nail. Problem is, I can't think of too many Christians who would actually be willing to compromise their middle-class comforts to welcome messy filth into their homes and hearts. That nail is just not hammered in deeply enough. That cross is just too heavy.

After more sleepless nights pondering these things in my heart, I arrive at no viable political answers to the gloom in the streets. In fact, I'm feeling more politically uncertain, tossed about, and up in the air than ever before. What I know for certain is that I will cringe whenever I hear anyone mandating that true Christians must vote for and support one party or the other. It's simply not that cut and dry. The two major parties both offer some promising political ideas, as well as some shortsighted detrimental ones.

We really can't know for certain what political action Jesus would take if he were an American today. He lived in a very different time and place. But we can drape ourselves with the essence of who he was and let that be our guide in all our decisions. And the essence of Jesus was to love those who seem impossible to love.

As philosopher and theologian John Caputo so eloquently puts it: "Jesus thought that when all the large and fine points of the Torah are taken into account, the law and the prophets come down to love of neighbor and of God, and he burned with anger when he thought the spirit of love was being undermined by inflexible rules or by hypocrisy. Love is the gift and love is not parsimonious. It does not dodge what is expected of it under the cover of rules or ideologies."

Love. Are we willing to love like this?

I turn in my two weeks notice. This line of work is not for me at this time in my life; it's obvious to me now. I need to be with real people, with real needs. I can no longer play the political game required on the Hill. I can no longer stand so committed to the Republican platform, nor can I bring myself to stand on the platform of the Democrats. The only platform I intend to stand on is that of Jesus, which, at this point, isn't looking like any of the political options. While I'm still unclear as to what the best political position is, given all the complexities, I'm certain of what my practical, on-the-ground faith response must be, and I will focus on pushing my feet in that direction.

Jesus is not a Republican, and this leaves another crack in my pot of certainties. So with my roots further pressing against my freshly-cracked vessel, struggling for more space, fighting for nutrients in the cramped quarters, I leave these halls of greatness. On my last walk back to Union Station, I cross paths with my old giggling friend, who I find faithfully rifling through a garbage can. I turn over my big black glasses to her. After fixing them to her face, she flashes me a toothless grin. I return the gesture and give my nod of approval. Once again, that silly schoolgirl laughter fills the space between us. I jubilantly declare: "Well aren't you the spittin' image of Jaclyn Kennedy Onassis!"

More giggles. I hear Jesus as I look across at this woman, "Whatever you do for the least of these, you do for me."

The journey from there takes me on a long, contemplative, winding road trip up the New England coast, salty air blowing in my windows, across my face, and tangling through my hair. Eventually, I cross over to Michigan and land at my parents' front door.

I apply for Seminary.

CHAPTER SEVEN

Plastering the Cracks

"WE ARE PLEASED TO inform you that you have been accepted into the Master's program at Calvin Theological Seminary." My letter of acceptance arrived.

I have no idea what I will one day do with this degree, but I figure it can't be anything but helpful to immerse myself deeply in the Text for a couple years. The trip to Israel was like a drop of honey on my lips, and I want more of it. I want to lap up the sweetness of the words of God, taste whole delicious mouthwatering bites of this dripping honeycomb. Regardless of what I do with the rest of my life, I know this will give me good grounding for wherever my path leads.

I move back into my parents' house in Holland, Michigan, and commute forty-five minutes to my graduate-level theological classes in Grand Rapids. This way I can work flexibly on their flower farm, squeezing in hours between Greek grammar, Anselm, and Augustine.

It's a bit of a challenge to be living back in the world that was once my home, my safe-haven. It now seems somewhat small, almost suffocating. Nothing here has changed, yet I've changed a great deal. In this place that once was so much a part of me, I now find a bit strange and myself somewhat strange in it. Those around me expect me to fall back into old roles, but I am no longer that person, and so there is a bit of tension—the twisting of cords between wanting to fall back into the old familiar self for the sake of comfort and convenience and wanting to assert my new less-certain-of-our-certainties self. Thankfully, I have school to keep me preoccupied.

I love the academic setting, love learning new things. I was one of those college students who switched majors seventeen times because I wanted to know more of everything, wanted to major in all subjects: from

English literature to sociology to archaeology to history to vocal performance to religion to art and everything in-between, with the exception of anything resembling mathematics, but finally settling with political science.

Books have been my constant companion. From childhood until now, I have had a deep love for the written word. My parents always had a bookshelf at the top of the stairs, and when I was young, I would lie on the floor, pulling books off the shelves. Not just the words on the page drew me in, but the very scent of them. I would spend hours lying there, flipping pages while the edges brushed against my nose. It was an experience that pulled in all the senses—sight, sound, touch, smell, and I swear I could even taste them.

Today, I'm often promiscuous in these relationships, having many love affairs going on with several books at one time, plowing through a handful in a week, underlining favorite passages, scribbling in the margins, and always eager to crack open the next one. I don't just devour books; I obnoxiously slurp them up and loudly smack my lips in the aftermath. The crumbs fall, and I refuse to sweep them up, and so the words lay everywhere scattered around me—on the sofa, at my feet, on the edge of the tub, stuck in the cracks between the floorboards, across the kitchen counters—everywhere bits of Dickens, Hemingway, Dostoyevsky, Plato, Augustine, Tolstoy, Steinbeck, and so many countless others who have risked themselves on the page, and who are now very much a part of my daily existence.

The bibliographies at the end of books always get me into trouble. If I like a book I'm reading, then I need to read many of the books referenced in that book. Then, in the reading of all those books, I have to add to my "must-read" book list all the books referenced in *those* books. And so my list quickly multiplies into a thicker and thicker compilation—a list that is capable of driving me to an unconquerable madness. Often I retreat to classic novels, which act as soft cushions, places of rest while the information in my head settles.

I used to dream of being a professional student, stacking up degrees until I was 65, at which time my student loans would be forgiven, and I could retire to a romantic life of writing in a cabin in the woods somewhere. More likely, this existence would have been a lonely life, a life never felt in the world, eventually culminating in dying an old maid with fingers crooked from constantly writing papers. Someone would probably find me a few days after the fact, pry the pen from my stiff digits, and chisel on my gravestone: "Here lies Christine: If you have any information on this woman, please contact the township supervisor."

In line for coffee and bagels at seminary orientation, I bump into a guy with bewitching Dutch delft blue eyes and a regal nose. His name is Bryan. We sit down and begin nibbling our bagels between mouthfuls of easy conversation. I discover that he's just returned from a year in Turkey evangelizing Muslim students, an experience which confirmed for him the call into ministry. And so he decided to get his Masters of Divinity. The more we talk, the more apparent it is that Bryan is not only a guy with an extremely sharp head but also a man with a deep love for God and a passion for understanding the biblical text.

Not long after our initial conversation, he calls and asks me out to dinner. Unfortunately, I have a conflict and tell him so. *Fiddlesticks*, I think, *of all the nights for him to ask me out.* He suggests another night, "Sorry. That won't work for me either," I explain, with sincerity.

"Okay." His voice clearly registers disappointment. We continue to cross paths at seminary and occasionally chat after class, but he doesn't broach the subject of asking me out again.

It's spine-tingling to once again be back in the classroom, to further study that which I've become so passionate about, to immerse myself in the Word of God, in order to be a more effective disciple.

In the meantime, I am invited on another study trip with the same teacher with whom I went to Israel—this time to study the early church in Turkey. With the approval of my professors to be absent for two weeks, I eagerly begin training for the strenuous hikes. A couple weeks before we leave, as my spirits soar in anticipation, suddenly, the world comes to a screeching halt.

While sitting in my *Philosophy of Religion* class, discussing and comparing Plato and Aristotle's idea of the Good, a school administrator steps in the door. The date is September 11, 2001.

The administrator solemnly whispers private words to my professor. The professor then enigmatically announces: "Something has happened." Mystery shrouds the class. Our professor silently dismisses the class. Having received little to no information on what is going on, we join with students from other classrooms and file into the auditorium. There, live

TV streams reveal unimaginable images of unimaginable history unfolding. We sit silent and dumbfounded as we watch the networks replay the video of the passenger jets descending and ripping into the Twin Towers, and eventually another into the Pentagon.

A paralyzing shock falls hard upon me. This is the stuff of movies and world history textbooks, not the sort of thing that happens in current, real life. A deep reticence claims the auditorium. Our eyes witness in-the-moment horror: those preferring to jump from 70-plus floors high rather than face the flames that must have been laying claim to their desks and cubicles. I could scarcely imagine it. *Did they have time to call their families and say goodbye? What goes through a person's head before he takes the leap that he knows will leave him in a thousand messy pieces on the sidewalk?* Nausea washes through me.

The auditorium begins to swell with tears, which rise up as incense, as prayers, as a communal crying out to God. An eerie coagulation of weeping and silence fills the room. Stunned disbelief. Prayers flood through my head: *Lord, have mercy on the thousands trying to escape. Guide them out of the darkness of the powerless towers. Comfort the waiting and worrying families. God do something! For the love of Christ, do something!*

Scattered around, some students quietly pray alone, some gather in small groups and whisper amongst one another, and others cling to another as if they, too, might get swallowed up in the crumbling world before us.

Our collective pleading to the Divine abruptly halts when interrupted with the inevitability of human engineering: Crunching of concrete. Twisting of metal and bodies. With and without fair warning, one of the towers comes crashing down, driving a storm of thick, blinding gray powder upon a choking New York City. I hold my breath, a subconscious gesture of empathy.

As the dust and rubble begins to settle, it seems the impossible has become a reality. Two of the most symbolically powerful structures known to modern man have toppled, dragging with them thousands of unsuspecting mortals, and the security of the most indomitable nation in the world. My mind races. *What is happening? Why would anyone do something so horrible to the United States of America, one nation under God? The nation who holds in its hand the power of life and death, the power to infuse peace where there is conflict, democracy where there is tyranny?*

With the auditorium lights dim, we sit in stillness among gray-blue hues flashing from the big screen, and the Towers' billowy smoke clouds mirror our blackest suspicions and questions. Eventually, students and professors peel their eyes from the chaos and somberly leave the room. I, and many others, exit the auditorium, sauntering the seminary halls in hushed whispers. We filter out through the doors and disperse to our cars like mere shadows of ourselves. I find it hard to divert my eyes to the forty-five minutes of pavement that leads me home to the TV screen in my parents' living room.

Living in the flight path of Tulip City Airport, the stillness of the skies over the next few days is like a memorial service, a long moment of silence held to remember those who had died, an extended prayer of rescue for anyone still trapped alive in the rubble. Time itself stands still.

The eyes of America become fixated on their televisions. We all hold our breath, certain that at least some survivors will be uncovered, will be given fresh air to gulp up into their dusty lungs. We need that. I'm certain that God will hear the crying out, the groaning of so many millions, for at least some to be found alive in pockets of rubble. He will surely give us some sort of graspable thing to feel hopeful about in these opaque days.

The rescuers find a few people alive here and there, but mostly, God seems silent. Where God is hushed, our Republican President, George W. Bush, is eager to step up and provide answers. His voice pours over my community like the balm of Gilead, soothing, alleviating the tempestuous vehemence rambling in our souls. Bush promises resolve. He promises to give back a sense of inner peace. He promises safety. He promises revenge. He tells us to keep shopping.

George W., who has been a mostly inconspicuous president up until now, is full of God-talk these days. Every action, every attitude, every word, appears justified by the consistent infiltration of the name of God into the suddenly confident speech of Bush. Everyone around me seems to feel comforted by his war-driven plan of action to retaliate. But all this God-talk mingled with "revenge" has me more than a little nervous, more than slightly uncomfortable.

I feel completely alone, as if trying to paddle my solitary kayak against the swift current of the dominating thought—a line of thinking that carries with it a whole fleet of vessels that continually pounds against me, pushes me downstream, drags me backwards, and pushes me under. I become overwhelmed to be surrounded by those—at home, church and seminary—who wholeheartedly affirm and justify every word, every deed, and every solitary breath of the President.

Condemnation quickly follows any slight hint of critique I offer or any question I raise—like I'm automatically an enemy against the force of Good. It becomes *them* against me. *They* push my words over, drown out my thoughts with what seems like a rehearsed rhetoric with a common theme of retaliation: "Kill those who killed us!" Shock. Disappointment. Fear. I can see it in *their* faces. I hear snippets of *their* disapproval. *They* say my love of country is sliding. *They* fear that my faith is on the edge of collapse. I begin to feel myself slowly slipping under the water, and the only hands I spot reaching for me, the only available rescue, comes from those who are reaching down from the fleet—the same fleet that pushed me under to begin with.

And so what can I do? I grab on as a means of survival. And so, in fact, it is *they* who lift me from the waters, wrap me in a warm blanket, and pamper me aboard this fleet of right-wing ships. When you're cold, wet and lonely, you'll warm yourself up to just about any idea as long as it ensures a sense of comfort and community. *Perhaps I was wrong to be so hard on the Republican party*, I force these thoughts, brainwash myself. *We are blessed to have such a Jesus-loving President*, I tell myself over and over.

The more time that passes, the more plausible *their* thinking begins to seem, that perhaps Jesus would be sporting an elephant bumper sticker on his donkey's rump, after all. Perhaps in Washington, my disapproval of the GOP was some sort of rebellious period, a season of clouded judgment, a time when I allowed the world to influence my worldview rather than my worldview to shape how I see the world. Could it be?

I find myself making excuses, grasping at justifications, listening to the voices that surround me, and, surprisingly easily, slipping back into old political philosophies. Life is just much more painless—even enjoyable again—when I nod and agree with those who are hedged in the same circles as me.

When I'm not talking about 9-11 with fellow students, I find myself listening religiously to the authoritative perspectives of Rush Limbaugh, Sean Hannity, and Glenn Beck while harvesting dahlias and trimming curly willow on the farm. The more I listen to conservative talk radio, the more feverishly I get worked up, the more I want to seek out those bastard Muslims hiding in caves myself and slowly blow their evil, soulless bodies to bits. *We will win this war on terror. God will win this war. Christianity will be the victor over Islam because God is on our side.*

At the close of October, a matter of the heart trumps all my anger and hatred. Well aware that I had bruised Bryan's ego with my previous declines, I gather he isn't going to put himself in the position of asking me out again, so I ask Bryan if he wants to study Greek together some time. One studying session leads to another, then another. Before long, we are lip-locked and in love. Love becomes a pleasant escape from the constant headlines buzzing with fearful words: Terrorism. Red alert. Insecure. Another posed threat.

After a few delightful months together, Bryan and I treat ourselves to a romantic dinner at a restaurant overlooking the Grand River. On a student budget, our date nights typically consist of ramen noodles, a few games of backgammon, and a cheap movie from the rental store. Rarely, if ever, do we get to eat at any sort of place requiring a tip. This night is going to be special. We get all dressed up to dream over a bottle of Merlot, filet minion cooked to juicy perfection, and tender-crisp green beans sprinkled with slivered almonds. We then finish the meal off with lightly toasted crème brûlée and creamed coffee. After our food settles, we decide on a slow stroll across the pedestrian bridge, under an impossibly perfect sky bursting with stars and a wink of the moon.

Nearly halfway across the bridge, Bryan nervously turns to me and grips both my hands in his. Instantly, I know what is about to happen. A girl dreams of this moment her whole life, practices it with her dolls a thousand times, scribbles notes about it in science class. A lump grows in my throat, and suddenly I can't breathe. Bryan drops down to one knee, blue eyes sparkling, hands shaking, and the poetry of Christina Rossetti splashing from his full lips. Tears stick to my eyelashes, blur my vision. My head is doing somersaults and I can scarcely make out what he is saying.

The next thing I hear are words from my own lips. "Yes! Yes, of course!" With a smile that spans the river, I accept his proposal. He slips a diamond on my finger. A week later, we begin plans for a summer wedding—a short engagement, we realize, but we're both approaching thirty and have dated enough to know a rare and good thing when we experience it.

As the impending wedding comes closer and the days grow painfully longer, Bryan and I busy ourselves finishing up the school year and trying to plan for a wedding and honeymoon that will somehow be sandwiched between summer classes. As seasons of life bring forth changes in nature, so too does that ring on my finger.

Unable to support ourselves if we both continue school, I decide to put my education on hold and work on the flower farm for the duration of Bryan's last three years of seminary. The sacrifice seems beneficial to this new season upon me. And it's actually not a second rate state of affairs. I thoroughly enjoy working with my hands, being outdoors among a variety of flowers in the warmer months. Autumn's red-orange color bursts make my soul sing, and the long arms of winter nudge me in to the warmth of the barn, where I trim and bundle curly willow, prepping for the freezer so they can maintain their freshness all year.

During these colder months, I sidle up close to the big three politically conservative talk show radio hosts. While the snows blow up against the side of the barn, these men keep me warm. Nine hours of repetitive work passes effortlessly under the alluring influences of these men whom I've come to respect as knowledgeable, wise individuals.

There is an addictive quality in the way they conjure up anger within me. They constantly remind me of how evil the world is and how good we are, a steady diet of self-assurance soup. We (American Christians) are good. They (Muslim terrorists) are evil. Good must blow evil to bits so that good might reign triumphantly in the world. If there is occasional hyperbole on their part, it is only to point out some larger truth.

Bryan and I decide to pinch pennies so we can afford satellite TV. We can't possibly trust the liberal news media to give a fair and balanced report of the war. As essential as oxygen, we simply must have *Fox News*— the big three say so—and the big three are never to be criticized (much like the holy Trinity). Just see what happens when someone calls into the radio show with an opposing view. Shark bait. These callers have nothing to stand on. Not a shred of a solid argument to support their anti-Republican positions. I find that I simply cannot trust any other network. As if nine hours of conservative talk radio isn't enough, now I have *Fox News* to play host to me in the evenings while Bryan studies.

Bryan begins to get a bit frustrated with some of the aspects of seminary. His passion for the Text gets buried deep under the heavy weight of theology. One day he comes home and drops his stack of books on the kitchen table. In exasperation, he asks: "Can you tell me why we have an entire semester-long class devoted to teaching us how to preach the Heidelberg Catechism? I'd so much rather spend that time studying and understanding the Text in its context!" He pulls out a chair and sits down. Deflated. Frustrated. "I mean, seriously, preaching from medieval doctrinal statements? Where is the power in that? Where is the life? It is the *text* that is living and active. That's what I went to seminary to study. That's what preaches!"

March 19, 2003: "Shock and Awe." With the warmth of a Pinot Grigio slipping down my throat, I observe with flat satisfaction the destruction of the Palace and Capitol buildings in Baghdad, certain that with every explosion, every blow of heat erupting into the air, some very powerful and very evil men are being eliminated. *Serves the bastards right.*

Or does it? That night I receive a surprise visit from my old nighttime companion: sleeplessness. Or perhaps it's the conscience coming to call. People come to mind. People with dark hair and dark eyes and dark skin. Muslims. Questions flood past the well-worn path of *Fox News* logic: *What's happening on the ground in Baghdad? What of the civilians who happened to be in the path of one of these flaming nightmares? How many died in the surprise attack? How many scream on hospital beds, skin melting, dripping off their bodies? Would we ever really know those numbers?* Then I consider: *Is slaughtering a bunch of people, destroying their infrastructure, really going to help us feel better about our own loss? How did we come to this point? Is there a hidden agenda—control of oil perhaps—that we've simply disguised under the veil of terrorism? Did we just need to unleash our anger somewhere, anywhere? Burst on the scene with guns blazing to send a message to the world that you better not mess with us?* Doubt creeps in like an uninvited guest, disrupting my certainties.

"Do not be overcome by evil, but overcome evil with good." That still small voice whispers to me in the night.

"Love your enemies. Pray for those who persecute you."

I'm stuck in mental muddiness. My own thoughts wrestle intensely with each other. Two sides internally throwing grenades at one another.

In church we pray for the war to be won. We pray for the success and protection of our soldiers. Everyone around me supports the war efforts. We're the good guys; they are the evil guys. No one in my Christ-loving, God-fearing community questions the President. In the eyes of those who surround me, our Republican President is a man devoted first and foremost to God Almighty, and so he *must* speak on behalf of God. You really can't question the actions of such a person. There's no room left for a voice of dissent, for a voice that criticizes any move made by George W. Bush. A voice like that, in a subculture such as this, would be laughed at, scorned, rejected. . . crucified.

On this particular night, I walk over to my vanity dresser and glance in the mirror, looking directly at my illuminated face and imagining what God himself might see. *Oh my goodness*, I say to myself. I realize that an ugly reality of myself has been festering, like an unnoticed and unattended cancerous growth. I've become a bitter person. Over time, I have re-adopted my little community's little philosophy that views itself as the *only* truth and the *only* goodness pitted against the purely evil world.

We are right, and everyone outside of our way of thinking is wrong. As we look out over the world, we have the God-given right to grumble and complain from the secure place of our narrow-minded rightness. Like my neighbors, I have again become smug and arrogant in my thoughts and beliefs.

My roots have begun to cramp and curl inward because this pot is allowing no room for outward growth. Some of the veins of my roots show signs of decline and begin to die. The plant is in danger of being stunted, of maturing at less than its beautiful potential.

Sleep never comes on this night.

In the Jewish tradition, when a person dies, there is a period of seven days where the family members sit in silence and mourn together. This is called *Shiva*. Friends come and visit to show their love and support for the family and their respect for the deceased. Contrary to the way we Westerners typically observe funeral home visitation in our culture—arriving with words of hope and assurance—during *Shiva*, Jewish mourners sit in complete silence, speaking only if spoken to by one of the close family members.

Now I wonder back to 9-11 when God seemed silent as the ashes of destruction drifted down slowly upon a terrified city while we raised our arms and cried out to him. Is it possible he was sitting *Shiva* with us? That God was there all along, silently beside us, lamenting with us in our pandemonium, choking down tears? Coughing up ashes?

Perhaps our President also should have sat in silence with us rather than boisterously promising revenge, eagerly pushing us on to business as usual, raucously cheering us on to hit the malls and slide our credit cards at store counters. If you are an ally of America, you should just shut up, listen to the President and go out and shop.

In the weeks ahead, I slowly pull back, refrain from watching the "War on Terror." I tune out of conservative talk radio and into silence. I excuse myself from participating in the discussions on the war that surround me every which way I turn. It's no longer within my conscience to support every action of the United States, yet my lone disapproval remains silent because I fear the backlash, the inevitable crucifixion.

And then again, comes the impassioned voice from the desert: "If you're going to call yourself a disciple, you better strive to walk as Jesus walked!" Fully ashamed of myself, and utterly disappointed, I realize that I'm just unwilling to do it, unwilling to swim against the strong current, unwilling to risk the nails in my hands and feet. While I feel our attacks on Iraq and Afghanistan may be wrong, I'm unwilling to stand up in my community and raise questions because I know uncomfortable repercussions will follow. Standing face-to-face with this self-realization becomes a devastating blow to my gut: *I'm a weak person.*

I continue to silently exist in this right-wing, conservative Christian world through the remainder of Bryan's seminary years. My passion for the Text is dwindling because I have a submerging suspicion of what I will encounter there, a hunch about what I will be called to do and say in my community. And, I now realize in my weakness, I will be unwilling to do it. I decide I'd rather live in ignorance of the Text because at least then I can go on living the status quo. Ignorance truly is bliss. Despite the tragedy of 9-11 and the country's distraction by "The War on Terror," life continues to go on.

After four grueling years of ancient languages, precision theology, and church history, Bryan's graduation day finally arrives. Bryan walks away with a gold-embossed certificate in his hand, verifying the Master of Divinity degree he has attained. Yet this paper represents a dueling match within Bryan, as he conveys to me a level of frustration about it all. He has enjoyed the in-depth study of languages and church history, yet laments: "After four years of intense study, I really didn't learn how to do theology, but rather how to regurgitate the assumed conclusive theology that had been decided 500 years ago." Additionally, he notes, study of the biblical text seemed handcuffed by the need to arrive at a very familiar, single interpretation of the Text. (See one such incident highlighted in Bryan's book, *Pub Theology*, Cascade Books, 2012). Yet Bryan has received tools to study the Text, that when fully utilized, will help us realize how far we've strayed from the path of Jesus. But here in this moment, the gold seal on Bryan's Master of Divinity parchment represents a straight and narrow line of accepted doctrine, marked in permanent ink, not to be edited nor erased.

And now the mission of Bryan and his fellow graduates is clear: Like a mother bird feeding her hatchling, they must spit out what they have just learned and plop it into the mouths of their various little flocks, comprised of docile little birdlings just waiting for food. The right food.

With seminary behind us, Bryan and I sense a new season has come upon us. We have a new life to create of our own; we are no longer entirely bound to past ideas of church, God, and life in general. We find that we have grown increasingly impatient with big, established church squabbles where small committees hash out such big problems: Should the carpet in the sanctuary should be beige or blue? Should worship be limited to the blue Psalter Hymnal, or should we incorporate the grey one? Do we dare to roll down a big screen over the cross? And these committees had looming concerns: Are Catholics going to hell? Should children be allowed to partake of communion? Should a woman (gasp!) be allowed to stand behind the pulpit?

These issues seem largely irrelevant to us, and as we discern our ministry calling, we realize that church planting might allow us to focus on the kind of ministry that we're passionate about. In anticipation of this, we meet with a lifelong church planter to hear the stories of the churches he started around the country—the ups and downs, the successes and failures, the joys and sorrows. We find ourselves drawn to the excitement and challenge of starting something new, something unknown. It seems refreshing to pastor a church with no historical congregational expectations held over us, and no old church baggage—luggage with gummed up wheels that no longer roll.

We attend an intense three-day church planter assessment, where denominational authorities test our skills, prod our personalities, counsel and evaluate us to determine if church planting will be a good fit for us. We pass easily, and excitedly pursue several new church plant opportunities.

Most commonly, a CRC church planter takes up a position to start a church where there's a group of former midwestern CRC folks already in place, people who've moved to a city and are incapable of imagining life without a CRC. These people contact the denomination requesting a church planter to help them start and grow a new church.

Another method of church planting is referred to as a "parachute drop," where a classis—a group of churches in a given area—determines that there are not enough CRCs in their region, so they hire a church planter. There are no people in place. Basically, the planter gets dropped off without knowing anyone or having any contacts in the area, and attempts to start a church from scratch.

We go through the interview process for two possible plants: Des Moines, Iowa, with a group already in place, and Traverse City, Michigan, as a parachute drop. Both extend a call to us, inviting us to plant a church in their area. We spend the next few weeks visiting the two locations, praying for guidance, listening, and waiting.

We *shiva*. Bryan and I sit silently together, gathered as mourners, saying goodbye to our past lives and waiting for God to reveal his next step for our future.

CHAPTER EIGHT

Going Deeper

As we drift through blissful blue skies, our parachute pops open and softly drops Bryan and I down in the land of endless sandy beaches, turquoise waters, rolling orchards, plump-ripe vineyards, and the home of Michael Moore's Film Festival. We have accepted the call to start a new church in Traverse City, a Midwestern, seasonal, tropical paradise. This should be smooth sailing.

During our first nine months in Traverse City, we immerse ourselves in the heartbeat of our new hometown. We focus on getting to know the people—the culture, the way they think, the way they live and what they value. During this time, we begin to determine our target demographic, location, strategy, etc.

After these months we have begun to tune into the ethos of life in Traverse City. Bryan and I then have the opportunity to receive additional training as church planters, so we excitedly attend an interdenominational church planting training conference, or "boot camp." So off we go to Indiana, where we learn—through bullet points, charts, graphs and statistics—the nuts and bolts of planting and growing a new church.

The boot camp trainers teach us their precise, tried-and-true church-planting Game Plan to Succeed:

Step 1: "You will begin the process by gathering people to yourselves, by any and all necessary means, in order to start a small group Bible Study. When your Bible study grows to inhospitable proportions, you will split into two home groups. When that becomes inhospitable, you will split into three groups, and this splintering shall continue until you have amassed around a hundred people."

Our Game Plan to Succeed lay before us, typed out, categorized and printed—simply and matter-of-factly—in beautiful charts and graphs. *I can follow this plan,* I acknowledge to myself, feeling good that someone else has thought this all through for me, practiced it, perfected it, and then given it to me in such organized fashion.

Step 2: "When you reach a hundred people, you are ready to worship together. If you meet for worship before you have a hundred, you will never get beyond those numbers. Time and time again, one hundred has been proven to be the critical number."

"Otherwise, you will *never* get beyond those numbers," the trainer repeats, pointing to the chart with a big, bold **100**. *Never* seems like a *really* long time. I don't want the people of Traverse City *never* to be able to worship together. That magic number 100 glues itself to my memory.

Step 3: "Once you get to a hundred people and worship together, you need volunteers: a welcoming crew at the door, another group serving coffee, fresh juice and gourmet cookies; several adults to manage the nursery; and adults to teach Sunday school for all the different age groups."

The phrase "worship together" lingers in my brain while the boot camp trainer's voice trails behind my thoughts: *We cannot worship together until we are a hundred people strong? Is that a fact confirmed in the Bible?*

My attention returns for a second heaping of Step 3: "Someone has to decorate the coffee table and the front of the sanctuary with floral arrangements. Everything needs to look pretty because this will set the tone for your (carefully constructed) worship service. If everything is pretty and delicious, people will keep coming back. Oh, and you'll need a prayer team to pray for you before, during, and after the service. And make sure you get some well-trained technicians in place to run the PowerPoint presentations, video productions, and sound."

I look at Bryan intermittently, for he often serves as my litmus test for the absurd. *Is this what we must do to start a church? Or is this ridiculous?* I vacillate, in silence. He seems to be concentrating hard. My brain begins to feel heavy, but in a surge to save the lost, I concentrate on whom our volunteers might be. I scan through the faces of the people of Traverse City that we have met thus far. I wonder: *Is Rob a well-trained technician? Would Becky make homemade cookies each Sunday? Might Leslie teach the children?*

I wonder how long my mind has been elsewhere, and I chide myself for being a lazy boot camp participant who simply cannot focus on the important task at hand.

Step 4: "You also need programs. Lots and lots of programs to create a niche for everyone's needs. People love programs. You need programs for children of all ages—programs for tweens, programs for teens, and programs for college-age kids. You need programs for singles, programs for married couples, programs for moms, and programs for the retired members. You need a men's sports club and a women's knitting group. You need programs for outreach and self-help book studies for in-reach. You need organizers and leaders for all those programs."

Programs! Programs! Programs! "Programs," I decide, is the catch phrase for the day. I keep waiting for the word "community" to pop up. Or maybe "friends." Or quite possibly "studying the Bible." *Maybe in Step 5*, I hope to myself.

Step 5: "You also need to prepare for a major launch service. Advertise! Advertise! Advertise that the circus will be in town entertaining the kids while the parents worship to the accompaniment of professional musicians, and the pastor spoon-feeds the masses with a feel-good message about God's love of the status quo. Advertise door prizes. Think big about door prizes. Think flat screen televisions for door prizes. People love door prizes. Door prizes and welcome baskets. Bait them with door prizes, and reel them in with great programs."

I can't tell if I have to throw up because of the mediocre cafeteria food I ate earlier or because of what the boot camp trainer continues feeding us. I sigh, assuming boot camp is over. But wait, there's more. Like an unnecessary P.S. to Tolstoy's 1,440-page *War and Peace*.

"Oh, and before you leave here, be sure to purchase our book and helpful packet of tools to guide your church plant down the right path to success. I guarantee that spending those couple hundred dollars will totally be worth your money!"

Whew! It's easy to see why we'd be in trouble doing the first service with fewer than a hundred people on board. After Bryan and I dole out all the responsibilities, no one will be left to sit in the pews! The comical thought of one hundred people working while the sanctuary sits empty makes me laugh. But my laughter soon shifts to concern. And even more quickly, to fear.

Bryan and I leave the training camp feeling like we've been dropped off at the bottom of Everest with no proper climbing gear and no climbing experience. We've nothing but a $200 travel guidebook called, *How To Climb Everest*, which seems largely unhelpful as we stand in the shadow of this colossal mountain range spread before us.

As Bryan and I head back to Traverse City—our Mount Everest, of sorts—one word looms over me like a dense cloud: Overwhelmed. Ready to give up before moving past *Go*. We try to digest all the information on the drive back to Northern Michigan, but serious heartburn and reflux result. The long ride is a mingling of silence, sighs, intermittent encouraging words, and then a few moments of: "What the dickens have we gotten ourselves into?" The landscape streams outside the car windows like a giant finger-smudged blur, mirroring the thoughts in my head.

By the time we pull into our garage, we decide that while the guaranteed success at boot camp seems too good to be true, *they* are the experts. They must know what they're talking about. We will give this plan a fair shot. We will enthusiastically push it with one hundred percent of our abilities. It's what we've been called to do, after all.

Over the next several months, Bryan and I try and try and try. We push and push and push. We endeavor to get this thing off the ground according to the boot camp's Game Plan to Succeed, utilizing all the strategic methods at our disposal. Every proven-to-be-successful trick of the trade. However, all this pushing and trying seems in vain, as all the strategic maneuvering results in little obvious success according to boot camp's measuring stick. Or any measuring stick, to be quite honest.

After nearly two years of striving to succeed boot camp-style, several people come and go from our group—the group that cannot worship together yet. People get tired of waiting for the magical number 100 so that we can have actual Sunday morning worship services.

Bryan and I plop down across from each other in the living room one night after the dozen or so people that we've managed to gather at this point have left for the evening. I sink in my leather chair, feeling deflated, exhausted, doubtful and discouraged. It's as if we've been running on a treadmill all this time, thoroughly fatigued but having gotten nowhere.

"What are we doing here?" I question aloud. "Why aren't our numbers growing as they so successfully and predictably rose on the charts in our boot camp workbooks? We have done everything—everything they told us to do. Maybe our initial church planter assessors were wrong. Perhaps we just aren't cut out for this."

Bryan, head back on his chair, sighs deeply, attempting to release the tension that seems to be squeezing him like a crafty boa constrictor. "Or perhaps we need to question the thing we're aiming for in the first place," he suggests.

"Which is what, again?" I truly can't remember the big picture, being so stuck in the thick of it.

"We've been trained to start a big church, performing the same Sunday song and dance as so many other churches in Traverse City." He looks at me with renewed intensity in those blue eyes that swooned me on the bridge. "Why are we doing that? Does Traverse City need another one of *those* churches? This city is inundated with that type of Sunday morning worship, as it is. If someone is looking for that, they can go anywhere, so why should we try to be like everyone else? Not to mention, there are probably half a dozen or so other church plants going on in this city, as we speak. I'm more interested in the *kind of community* we want to have. Something where we know each other and where people can be real. Where we engage the Text together. Frankly, I don't care how many people we have. In fact, less might actually be more."

"All right. So what do you think we should do, then? Just start Sunday morning worship?"

"Yes. I think we should just start Sunday morning worship." He is serious.

"Start Sunday morning worship? With four families?"

Silence. I chew on my bottom lip as I consider his suggestion. It actually makes a lot of sense. Bryan can teach, which is his strong suit as well as the thing he's most passionate about. But I can't shake the sharp warnings from the leaders at boot camp. "What about the numbers? They warned us over and over about the disastrous results of starting worship too early. If we start too early, it will never get off the ground. They were very firm about this." I slice my hands through the air as if to draw some imaginary definitive line. "We can't worship until we have a hundred people," I remind him.

Bryan raises his eyes. "Where two or three are gathered. . ."

"Oh, come on, what does that have to do with church planting? We both heard what the church planting experts told us, emphatically!" Even as I say it, I realize the absurdity of my own words, more evidence supporting the fact that it's always best for me to think about things a bit before I speak.

Bryan laughs under his breath and, ever the wiser one, says nothing. And so my foolish words linger in the air and ring in my ears, producing an uncomfortable silence, allowing those words to penetrate the recesses of my mind. Good grief.

It doesn't take long for me to agree. "Okay. What the dickens? Let's do it," I concede. "I guess at this point, we have nothing to lose, right?"

It is now mid-summer, and we decide to give Sunday morning gatherings on the beach a try. We'll give this plant one last push through the summer. If nothing comes of it, we'll pull out. At this point, we pretty much expect it to fail. Bryan begins to dream of going back to school, getting a PhD and teaching somewhere. Graduate school brochures begin arriving in the mail.

After some discussion, we decide at a group gathering that we will call our little church "Watershed." A watershed is a body of water—sometimes seen, sometimes unseen—that brings life to the area. Our vision for this church, if it ever becomes such, is to be a fluid flowing in and through Traverse City, bringing life wherever we go, in whatever we do, whether seen or unseen.

I have just recently given birth to Charles Frederick, our third baby boy in four years time. I'm exhausted. Exhausted from babies and church planting. The emotional highs of a beautiful new baby mixed with the lows of poopy diapers, sleepless nights, and a seemingly failed church plant attempt, run me ragged. Add to this the ridiculous amount of brain cells that dissipated with each baby I pushed into the world, and I'm plain tuckered out. Perhaps it would have been easier to just take a call to an established church—a church with good programs, a church with a good *nursery* program. *Soon this will all be over,* I remind myself, *and we will move on to something more normal.* I convince myself to enjoy all that summer in Traverse City has to offer—the many festivals, the sandy beaches, the hiking, the extensive orchards and rolling vineyards, and the quaint downtown with all its local specialty shops.

Our first gathering on the beach begins. Four families show up, including ours. Thank God, one person comes with a guitar strapped on his back.

We sing a few songs and Bryan does some teaching. The singing is rough on the edges, but also very organic feeling. Surprisingly, I find that I actually like worship this way, raw and unrehearsed. It's completely lacking the big shiny band, the electrified, PowerPoint laser-light-show sort of experience. The kids, armed with plastic shovels and pails, keep themselves busy with castle construction and serious excavation of moats.

The teaching time is powerful. Bryan has recently returned from Israel, where he had been on a study tour similar to mine. He decides to take advantage of our lakeside setting to teach one of the lessons from the Galilee region. It's effective. I find myself marveling at the teaching capabilities of my husband. *He was born to teach*, I muse to myself. *He's an absolutely brilliant communicator.* My gut instinct tells me we're on to something.

The few that show up also share how natural, authentically worshipful, and intimate the whole encounter feels. A renewed excitement begins to rouse within me for what we are here to do. I realize I want the whole city to experience what took place on this beach. So we make up some posters and spend the week placing them around town—on storefront windows and coffee shop bulletin boards.

Sunday comes around again, and the same three families show up and settle in beside ours. Disappointment sets in. It's hard to enjoy worship fully on this day because reality stampedes my expectations for a larger crowd. The only thing that keeps us from giving up just yet is that summer in Traverse City is like an extended stay in a tropical paradise. It makes the bitter reality that we were failing a much easier pill to swallow.

I often take my sulking to the beach, a short walk from our house. As my body slips, glides, and streamlines through the clear turquoise waters, under a yawning blue sky with the warmth of the summer sun on my face, the natural beauty has the effect of dissolving all my disappointing realities. The beach provides constant refreshment and renewal to my soul. The water has become my magical cure-all drug. I self-prescribe a daily dose, even if it's only for a quick dip.

In the meantime, our supporters keep asking us about the numbers. Numbers, numbers, numbers. Must it always be about the numbers? With little understanding of church planting, our family and friends from back home also measure progress by membership quotas. Always the question: "How many this week?" comes our way. By this standard, we constantly feel as if we are failing. But the more our small group gathers, the more intimate and deeper we go with each other. Never have I experienced such a living, breathing authenticity with fellow worshipers. Something beautiful happens on these Sunday mornings—an intricate combination of experiences—our time together is challenging, refreshing, engaging, real and unbound, all at the same time. Over the summer, I slowly begin to relax more and more on Sundays, fully immersing myself in our little organic worship time as I forfeit expectations of a big crowd.

Despite the intimacy of the worship, we realize such a small community will never be self-sustaining. And so, with two Sundays left in the summer, we begin to think about how to announce our "failure" to our beach congregation, our supporters, and the denomination, as well as consider where we will move to next, what we will do.

The second-to-last Sunday arrives, and we prepare to worship with the same four families, including ours. This morning, I wake early to nurse Charles. The wide open windows and the quiet comfortable morning air, yet undistracted by the daily disturbance of human activities, softly blows over me. In this silent house, before the Sunday morning chaos ensues, I whisper up a few words to God. "Listen, I realize we're no experts at this. We have tried our best to be faithful with what we have, with what we know. It's truly my desire to bring people to you in a deep and meaningful way. And while we may be viewed as failures by those on the outside because our numbers are stagnant, it has for me, been a really beautiful experience to discover and worship you so deeply and intimately, in community with these people. We've given you our best, but it may not be enough to keep this thing going. If you want the Watershed community to continue, you're just going to have to step in here. I'm giving it up to you. If this is not your will, then I accept it and will rest in knowing it."

This morning, as I throw down our blanket on the beach and set up a couple beach chairs, a new couple shows up. This is unexpected. Then another couple saunters over with their beach chairs. And they keep coming. So many blankets, bibles, and beach chairs. I can't believe it. Over twenty people show up! The sky paints a picturesque mixture of blue and contrasting white wisps; the breeze is just soft enough to keep us alert and comfortable.

Worship is powerful with all these voices echoing off the bay. People write furiously during Bryan's message, taking down points to remember. Children frolic up and down the beach, their laugher a natural backdrop to this terrestrial setting containing our earthy, organic worship.

Lingering afterwards, nearly every new person begins to enthusiastically remark that this is exactly the sort of experience they have been searching, praying, and longing for. It seems that in the eleventh hour, just as we were about to pull the plug on this church plant, God has stepped in.

With renewed excitement, we gather the following Sunday. Everyone returns, and some of them have brought their friends. Suddenly, a sense of momentum grows. This little community begins to roll like the waves that witness our worship.

The winds shift. The tilt of the earth decreases the directness of the sun, and turns the leaves to hues of browns, releasing them from the grip of the branches. Fall arrives. We head indoors, meeting weekly at a rented space in a partially renovated, previously abandoned state asylum with a somewhat shady history. We slowly pick up a few new families over the winter, most of them drawn to Bryan's teaching of the Text that includes the historical, cultural, and linguistic context. These teachings arrive like a fresh breath, blowing dust off the ancient words. Words that had been so familiar to us all our lives now take on new life, with a penetration that sinks deep and takes root in our very souls. In time, our community becomes more than a Sunday morning event, more than three points to discuss over coffee. Church expands to encompass a holistic philosophy of life, a way of living and worshiping with every single breath, well beyond Sunday mornings. As a faith community, together we seek to embody Jesus in tangible ways to all those we encounter in the larger Traverse City community and beyond.

Surprisingly, despite our increasing numbers, we have somehow managed to maintain that rare authenticity, participating fully in each other's joys, sorrows, and struggles. No one is perfect here. No one even pretends to be perfect. People lay it all down, and together we discover and experience forgiveness, encouragement, deep healing, and fellowship. That first step toward authenticity, involving deep vulnerability, is positively terrifying. But what results is a most unexpected composition of peace, love, support, and a raw, honest worship that extends beyond the songs we sing or the sermon preached.

More and more, less-than-perfect people walk through our doors each Sunday morning, such a contrast to the church atmosphere in which I grew up. We begin to attract sinners simply because we are all so obviously and tangibly such. People express that they've been tired of pretending, tired of glossing over a multitude of struggles and sins with a Sunday smile. They find Watershed to be a home, a place to empty themselves, to let go of the heavy bags they've been toting around. They are filled instead with hope, peace, love, and goodness. Now, when they are out in their neighborhoods and workplaces, all that goodness starts to naturally flow from them.

Others arrive with deep festering wounds from past church experiences. Some are tired of over-imposing church hierarchies impeding on the work of the Holy Spirit. Others have come exhausted from being guilt-driven slaves to the many programs that often hold churches hostage. Some express frustration with the larger, systematic hypocrisies contained and unquestionably accepted within the walls of their former churches. And while even this community has its own failings, we try our best to be honest about them.

Overall, many have come seeking simplicity and healing. While Bryan's contextual and historically-rooted messages often go deep, the message is as simple as this: "The world is broken. You and I are broken. And Jesus has arrived announcing that a new way is at hand. That healing is ready to begin." As disciples of Jesus, we seek to receive this healing and embody Jesus—demonstrating this love to the world around us—a love that lays down its life, even for its enemies. We seek to understand who Jesus was in his context and how it applies to our lives today.

We decide that even as our numbers grow, with the exception of nursery and children's worship, we will refrain from creating programs at Watershed unless absolutely necessary. We don't want to exhaust people on church commitments. We also realize that many good things are happening in the community already, and rather than reinvent the wheel, we encourage people to get involved in the opportunities that already exist. We intentionally focus on bringing *shalom* to the chaos that exists in the most natural places in our lives—in our places of employment, our schools, our homes, our neighborhoods, and our relationships.

Rather than trying to draw the world in to Watershed, we want to send the people of Watershed out into the world. It isn't about growing a big church for the sake of having a big church. It isn't about getting people inside the doors of the church building (or in our case, the insane asylum), but rather it's about being the living church to people outside our doors. It's about bringing the *shalom* of Jesus to the chaotic world in which we find ourselves, in very real and tactile ways.

"Go deeper," Bryan reminds us every Sunday morning. "Deeper with God, deeper with each other, and deeper in the world around you."

Chapter Nine

Compost

During the winter, I discover Shane Claiborne's book, *The Irresistible Revolution: Living as an Ordinary Radical.* This man, and the life of service he's living, reminds me again of my call as a disciple of Jesus. Shane describes an authentic faith rooted in belief, action, and love. But Shane's book is unique in the sea of so many books on living faith because not only does he teach us with his words, but he shows us radical love with his hands and feet.

He's living in the midst of chaos, bringing *shalom*. He walked with Mother Theresa for a time, dressing the weeping wounds of lepers. He sat with Iraqi families while our U.S. bombs exploded around them, splintering their lives and livelihoods into a hundred thousand pieces. With a few friends, he dumped $10,000 in cash on Wall Street to personally (and literally!) redistribute his wealth. He relocated and settled himself into one of the most impoverished communities in our nation, a neighborhood in North Philadelphia, to live among and love the homeless, the destitute. He brings life and a living, breathing resurrection to those who are the most neglected, the most pushed aside, the most feared, the most criticized, and the most ignored. He is doing it. He's a living, walking disciple like few others ever will be, and he inspires me.

Poring over the thoughts and stories of this remarkable ordinary radical, I feel a sharp prick to my conscience. I stand face-to-face with the realization, once again, that I am a fairly inactive believer, rarely making any real sacrifice to be the hands and feet of Jesus. The passion to follow in the footsteps of Jesus, which stirred up within my soul in Israel, has waned over time. The prayer for "eyes to see" rarely even passes by as a thought in my mind. Even though, as a community of believers, we spread *shalom* to places of chaos in Traverse City, I realize that it isn't really costing me anything. I help people out when it's convenient for me. I give out of my abundance, but rarely do I give of my first fruits. I'm living the American Dream. But I begin to realize that it's not my dream. Nor God's, I imagine.

"Take up your cross and follow me." What is the cross I bear?

I can't help now but to examine my life sharply and critically—my goals, my passions and how I spend my time, money, and energy. I recall something Cornelius Plantinga, one of my Calvin College professors once said to me: "What we do with our time and resources reveals everything about where our loyalties lie."

What happened to the girl who sat with the homeless, wiped vomit from the face of the drunks, and passed out PB & J's with TLC? Have I allowed this very settling, comfortable, middle-class life—in this very settling, comfortable, middle-class town—to clutch me firmly with its ideologies of consumerism and contentment with the status quo? What do I do with all the hours of my days? Where does all the cash in pocket end up? It's painful to think about, agonizing to take an honest look at my life as I attempt to answer these questions.

I can't stop thinking about Shane Claiborne and the tremendous impact that a single, radically faithful man has had in the world. At times, absorbing Shane's words feels to me like an annual physical—the full body physical—the one with the pap smear. It's awkward and uncomfortable. It's borderline invasive but also a necessary process to go through in determining my health, or in this case, my spiritual health.

Typically the doctor's assessment is something like: "You're in great shape. Could use a little more iron in your diet, but otherwise, in great shape." But this book doled out a more dim prognosis, a deeper look at the interior: "Um, let's see. . . you need to lose forty pounds, you have a dangerous deficiency in vitamins, your liver is beginning to rot, and the irregularity of your bowel movements suggests you're eating too many Cheezy Twists and spending too much time sitting on your rump. You're at risk for heart disease, diabetes, and high blood pressure. If you don't make some changes in your lifestyle real quick-like, death will be knocking on your door."

To maintain a physically healthy lifestyle, it's important to have a steady, balanced intake of nutrients. But also important is that we get adequate exercise, to exert the energy we've consumed, lest it turns to fat and begins clogging our arteries and downgrading our overall health.

Looking back, I've been consuming God my whole life, yet how much have I actually exercised that knowledge? How much have I applied it to my life? Sure, I have faithfully placed my tithe in the collection plate as my neighboring pew sitter passed it along to me, I sang in the choir, taught Sunday School, and participated in endless other churchy do-good activities throughout my life—*within* the church walls. Not that these are bad things at all; I am grateful we have people who do them. But I, personally, keep sensing a call to something else, something different.

How much have I actually lived the way Jesus lived? With the possible exception of my time with the homeless in D.C., it seems I've been a couch potato Christian for most of my life, spiritually lazy, largely content to sit on my faith beside other Christians in my cozy surroundings, unwilling to sacrifice comfort as I rattle off the five points of T.U.L.I.P. As I examine the inner workings of myself, I begin to wonder and question: *Is there something in my theology that creates this attitude? Something in my politics? Something in my culture? Some combination of them all?* This stream of ponderings takes up residence in my head, unpacks its suitcase, and shows no signs of moving out.

I allow myself to imagine for a moment whole groups of comfortable Christians moving to an impoverished community together. I imagine a generous outpouring of love on those so desperate for it. An embodiment of the Spirit of God. *What would this community look like? What would happen to the neighborhoods? Would the power of God transform them in unexpected ways? Would we find ourselves radically transformed as well?* What if every "follower" of Jesus took up walking his path in a radical way—down to the gritty, smelly details? Would the *whole world* be transformed? Would everyone on earth be so completely blown away by such an unfathomable, selfless, gracious kind of loving that they couldn't help but to be swept up in the movement themselves?

I wonder if all our inside church squabbles and heated debates on the fine points of doctrine and theology result from too much energy contained within our walls, and not enough going out. That pent-up energy must erupt somewhere, in some way. It seems that when congregants get involved in mission projects together, expending their energy on helping those outside, the inner conflicts tend to cease. Perhaps there's something in our faith that needs to be faced with real needs of real people. Could it be that in channeling our energy outward, a dissolving of inner differences naturally occurs? Does unity prevail when we focus on serving others?

Nighttime thoughts, once again, march into my once-cozy brain with cymbals and trumpets and flutes and bass drums and even a big ole' tuba—blasting away at my serenity. Good grief. Why is it that every time I begin to settle in my hammock and get comfortable in life, someone comes along with a big stick and starts poking at me? Why? Do I do this to myself, or is some larger force prodding me? The questions turn inward: *What am I willing to risk? What comforts am I willing to give up? What sort of cross am I willing to carry?*

An enthusiasm wells up in me, a desire to be stretched, prodded, challenged, and forced to think outside the soils in my cracked pot. I contemplate an alternative way of living, apart from the corrupt economic and political systems that seem overwhelming to anyone seeking real change. I conclude that settling into a chaotic neighborhood and spreading *shalom* with a Jesus-following, socialist-minded Christian community, might possibly be a powerful way to transform lives for Jesus, including mine.

I begin the long process of educating myself on the nuts and bolts of our economic system and the alternative world economy of fair trade. I learn about living with less, in contrast to the hyped-up world around me that utilizes every means of communication to convince and brainwash me into believing that I need more. This is the way of our capitalist, consumer-dependent economy. In a nutshell, our corporations ship all their production overseas to developing nations (driving millions of Americans to unemployment), rape their environmental resources (little environmental regulation exists in these parts of the world), and exploit the men, women and children there, holding them at a high level of desperation (so they will always work for pennies, or worse). All this so I can have more and more cheap stuff, a bunch of stuff that is built with a limited life expectancy so I'll soon need to buy more stuff. But obviously, for people on the other side of the world, the cost of all my inexpensive stuff is very high. Very, very high, indeed. The fate of much of my broken stuff is that it will be shipped back to these third world nations and dumped into massive, unregulated, stinking, disgusting heaps. Out of sight, out of mind. At least for us, for now.

I also learn about alternatives to participating in this system of environmental exploitation and degradation of people groups around the world. When I make a fair trade purchase, the money goes directly to the person whose hands lovingly crafted that item, rather than to the executives of a major corporation, with pennies trickling down to assembly line workers somewhere in Asia or Central America. Often fair trade items cost more, but if I can ignore the billboards and advertisements and seek contentment with less, my purchase will be made with the good of the world in mind, not just a purchase for my temporary entertainment to the detriment of some poor soul in Thailand and the often irreversible destruction of the planet. Shopping fair trade seems like a beneficial way to help those who struggle around the world in a very real and life-changing way.

I find myself counting sheep again, as I continually contemplate the nature of our economic system. Sleep refuses to come. I wonder, wrestle, and tackle the question of the role of faith in economics. In my right-wing world, Christians often equate fair trade and environmental responsibility with liberalism. Liberalism, of course, equates with Satan and his dark angels. Now, obviously, you don't have to be a liberal to support fair trade or environmental responsibility. Yet I wonder: *As a Christian, shouldn't I be leading the pack in promoting alternatives such as fair trade? Shouldn't I be on the front lines in the fight for justice and mercy of various exploited people groups around the world? Shouldn't I be pushing for healthy environmental stewardship, to care for all the world, as God mandated?* It seems that in the intimate intertwining of conservative political-economic perspectives with our faith, we've become incapable of making necessary distinctions, no longer able to separate what is truly good and desired by God from what is not.

Give me eyes to see.

Becoming more aware of the systems in which I participate encourages me to consume less and to become a more conscious consumer. But this new awareness further severs me from my right-wing upbringing, where the free market is somehow equated with—and necessary for—experiencing and expressing our God-given free will. When I bring up terms like "fair trade," "organic," or "social justice" in discussions with people from my hometown, they cringe. Many automatically assume that I must be a Democrat, a cheerleader on Satan's squad. I am neither. But I am left with a myriad of questions, wondering what sort of faith tradition would place these labels on someone who authentically seeks justice and mercy, who desires to follow Jesus, and who desperately wrestles with seeking eyes to see what God sees.

For the most part, I grew up in a community that assumed the poor are poor because they are lazy. A hard work ethic is paramount. The harder you work, the more you get, and the more you deserve. It's just that simple. God helps those who help themselves (a statement I can't seem to find anywhere in the Bible, by the way). But Jesus clearly states that his disciples must care for those who are in need. Period. He also speaks out against the unjust systems that create that poverty in the first place. Justice is paramount for Jesus. This seems to be, in fact, one of the things his heart is most concerned with.

When it comes to money and storing up the things of this world, Jesus speaks words of caution and condemnation. But somehow, at the same time we read these biblical words, we ignore the cries of the poor, holler at them to get off their lazy asses and get a job. All this, on our way to the mall so we can pick up the latest, trendy, made-in-Thailand outfit to replace last year's "so not happening" made-in-China attire. *How did we come to this point? What sort of gospel have we embraced? Where is the connection between what we believe and how we live out our everyday lives?*

I need a vacation from all this thinking and wrestling. I'm tired. I want to cruise through life. I don't want to think about everything so much. I'm tired of questioning the way things are. Why can't I just accept how the world works? Why can't I succumb to the fact that the current flows this way and then hop on my inner tube and just float? What's wrong with me? Maybe I should stop reading so much—sell all my books and purchase a TV. I don't want to know anymore. I want my ignorance back. Life was so much simpler when I was living in oblivion. *Drums, trumpets, tubas, please go away! You make too much noise in my head!*

Perhaps we ought to remove ourselves from the larger systems as the Amish or Mennonites do. A simple, uncomplicated life. Yet a Reformed worldview suggests some level of involvement. But how much do we seek to influence politics and economics, and to what end? Is it worth our time and energy seeking to change the larger corrupt systems that sometimes create poverty and take advantage of the destitute? On the other hand, how can we stand by and do nothing? As participating citizens of the larger American community, don't we have an obligation to expose and to speak out against the injustices we see?

Or ought we to simply leave the corrupt systems alone, lest we get too enmeshed and become corrupt ourselves? Should we work tirelessly to embody the kingdom of God (not to be confused with America) alongside—and in the midst of—these looming systems? Or can we effectively usher in the kingdom from *within* the broader economic systems? Should we seek to put ourselves in positions of power to change those systems that lead to socio-economic injustices? But then so many politicians who already serve in those places—and who identify themselves as followers of Christ—push for the very systems that lead to that disparity in the first place.

I fear I'll never sleep again. I begin to think that I'll probably, in fact, die of sleeplessness. I know I'm powerless to fix it all, but at least I must do my part. I want to do the right thing, to make the right choices, to be a truly conscious consumer. I start to go crazy at the store, reading labels, doing extensive research before every purchase, wanting to know exactly where my stuff comes from, learning about the conditions of the workers who assembled the products, and knowing where the large corporations are investing their massive earnings. It's an extremely daunting and discouraging process as I come to realize the near impossibility of completely stepping outside of the larger systems. And so I settle for promoting justice when and where I can, in purchasing fair trade, used, and locally made items. But I continue to purchase products beneficial to the large corporations as well because I find it an exhausting impossibility to step completely outside of these looming systems.

The prevailing American attitude towards economics seems contrary to the community-focused attitude of sharing everything with anyone who has need, which the first followers of Jesus promoted. Have we lost sight of truth? Have we dismissed the message of the cross? Have we buried it, or perhaps covered it with the American flag? Do we value individualism over community? Do we treasure profits over people? Is our fight for lower taxes selfishly motivated? Are we more concerned with getting more stuff—the latest, biggest and best of stuff—at the expense of the earth we've been mandated to maintain?

The bottom line question again becomes this for me: Have my attitudes of faith bled into and affected my economic and political attitudes, or have I allowed my political and economic attitudes to bleed into and persuade my faith?

I realize the obvious answer, and I curse myself for it.

I stand here, frustrated, staring at the inconsistencies of my religious experience, unable to sort out the message of Jesus effectively and clearly from the message of our capitalist economy. Perhaps in the wealthiest nation on the planet where over-abundance is the norm, we remain absolutely clueless about what it is to take up our cross. If we're asked to shoulder some of the financial burden for those in need, we sometimes respond by shaking our fist and rising up, and it seems to me there is something absolutely unChrist-like about that.

I sink down into my leather reading chair, scanning the room and its abundance of a comfortable life lived, and I ask myself, *Christy, do you want to follow the Jesus of the Bible, or do you want to be on the heals of the American Jesus?*

The trumpet blows. The war within starts anew, pushing me to new, uncomfortable places. Unknown, uncharted territories beckon me to explore. The tide of change is washing upon me, like it or not.

CHAPTER TEN

Uncovering Roots

ROOTS. NEARLY FORGOTTEN.

Like some gnarled apple tree, we enjoy the plump fruit. We adore the Maker for the splendor of the timely changing of her garments from fragrant white to green to orange to red to rust. Then we stare with envy at her confident naked form, curving against the cold winter winds, a stark contrast to the white of the swirling snows. But rarely do we think about the roots. Rarely do we stop to appreciate the strength, the depth, and the beauty of the many fingers of the hidden base that twist down through the earth—becoming entangled in the dirt and muddled in the mire—and hold the tree in its place. The roots grasp at vitamins, minerals, and water entrenched in the soil, absorbing them and pushing them upward to nourish the many branches.

Without the roots, no tree survives.

The roots that push down define the branches that have pushed up and out. Damage the roots, and you've broken the channels that carry life to the branches.

So, what are the roots of our Christian faith? The Hebrew Scriptures. The ancient Jews. Certainly our roots must give sustenance to the branches of our faith. With great interest in Old Testament studies, Bryan and I decide to begin a Torah Study group. We want to understand the roots of the New Testament faith, to understand the context of the world in which Jesus lived. The more we study, the more we find ourselves convicted to live into the Jewish Festivals for a year, as a way to understand and to appreciate more fully the biblical world and the roots of our faith.

We discovered this contextual study to be a beautiful, powerful way to experience a small piece of the faith Jesus himself practiced. We studied the ways that Jesus himself participated in the festivals. How he embodied them, and—as understood by some of the early Christian writers—fulfilled them. Celebrating the Jewish feasts and festivals of our heritage, in light of Jesus, provides a powerful connection to the depth of my faith. It's absolutely beautiful, for example, sitting in our temporary shelter, or *sukkah,* around a low table at a meal with friends, practicing ancient hospitality, retelling the story of the desert wanderings, sleeping under the stars, and imagining life in the desert and on the move. Jesus' life and teachings gain depth and texture when I dig deeper into his world, and they come alive as I live into some of these ancient Jewish practices. Yet new questions begin to swirl around in my mind.

Why does Christianity almost entirely ignore the Jewish calendar? When did we stop observing these festivals? Why are my family and friends so frantically upset and concerned that we are suddenly "acting Jewish"? Jesus becomes so much richer and more meaningful to me in this fuller context, and meanwhile, everyone tells me how extremely "dangerous" it is to flirt with Judaism.

"Christy, don't you know that Jesus fulfilled the Old Testament so we don't have to do it anymore?"

Yes, I've heard this many times in my life. *But what does that really mean?* I wonder. As I dig around in the original language, it turns out that the word "fulfill" doesn't mean the law is "finished," as I've always assumed. Rather, it means that Jesus lived the law perfectly. As his disciples, we are supposed to live as he did. He showed us how to live perfectly, so does this mean I ought to be Torah observant as well?

The Ten Commandments, I discover, are a summary of the Torah. Growing up, we heard those from behind the pulpit every Sunday in church. So perhaps, in a way, we attempted to live the Torah without even realizing it. But then Jesus goes on to further summarize the Torah in a single and most important law: love.

Love. Love for God. Love for neighbor. If it's this simple, why such a strong focus on and need for the incredibly complicated and intricate doctrines and theologies I believed my whole life? Why do Christians so often neglect Jesus' law of love, in exchange for hurling condemning insults at those who differ in the particulars of theology? The "why" questions become increasingly important to me.

I discuss some of these questions with a friend over coffee and blueberry scones one morning. She relays the following story to me:

There once was a woman who always cut the ends off her roast
before lovingly placing it in the roasting pan. One day her
husband asks her, "Why do you always cut off and throw
away the perfectly edible ends of the roast before you put it
in the pan?"

"I don't know" she replies matter-of-fact, "because that's is how
my mother always cooked a roast."

She phones her mother. "Mom," she asks, "why do you always cut
off the ends off the roast before putting it in the pan?"

"I don't know," she responds," because that's what your Grandma
always did."

The woman decided to pay Grandma a visit in the nursing home.
"Grandma," she asked, "why did you always cut the ends off
the roast before putting it in the roasting pan?"

"Because," she said, "my small roasting pan was never big enough
to squeeze in the whole roast."

I want to know who cut the Jewish roots from the Christian roast, and
what the original motive was for doing so. Is it something we do simply because it's what the generation before us did? Can we reach our growth potential and full measure of beauty and fruitfulness if we neglect our roots?

I want to understand why I believe what I believe. I want to grasp
the significance of it all. I want to believe what I believe because I really
and *truly* believe it, not just because it's what my parents believed. Too
many things begin to seem inconsistent, and it's not sitting well with me.
I've become uncomfortable with the matter-of-fact black and whiteness
of every issue, and of every aspect of God. It seems more and more that
things are far more complicated, that they settle somewhere in the grey,
that the possibilities of ways in which one can connect with God are endless. I decide on a necessary voyage back through the annals of Christian
theological history—the history that formed my theological assumptions.

I spend days in the library, scouring the bookcases for credible
sources, checking out every book I can get my hands on. My hungry
eyes read constantly, determined to get to the bottom of this, to journey
to the very base of what I believe. My face disappears, swallowed by my
books—at the beach, in bed at night, at mealtime, while I scrub floors,
fold laundry, and nurse my babies. Always I'm turning pages, seeking the
answers. Always, page, after page, after page.

~ ~ ~

This search to discover when and why Christianity was severed from its Jewish roots leads to several shocking encounters with scandal along the way. I'm disturbed by the things I uncover in my church history.

One of the places I see on my little tour back in time, which causes me to lose sleep, comes just after the year 300 A.D. It is October 27th, 312—just about exactly 1700 years ago—when a young Roman general looks to restore unity to a severed Roman Empire. Ruling in the north, he makes plans to take over the territory of Maxentius to the south. On this date, he looks out across the Tiber River and realizes he is terribly overmatched. He cannot win. According to legend, he falls asleep that night and has a dream. The myth varies, but the consensus is that he sees a vision of a cross in the sky at night, with the Greek words, *En toutō níka,* usually translated into Latin as, *in hoc signo vinces,* both phrases meaning: "in this sign, [you shall] conquer." Others say he saw a vision of a *chi rho,* an early Christian symbol, a monogram of the first two Greek letters in the name Christ. In any case, the general takes this as a sign from God— or the gods—and emblazons crosses on his standards, perhaps with the initials *ihs* (*in hoc signo*). In an incredible and fateful moment of history, this young general crosses the Milvian Bridge, somehow fights through to Maxentius, who in the battle falls from his horse into the river and drowns.

The general's name: Constantine. The first Roman Emperor to "embrace" Christianity. But what I discover, as I read, is that this was a calculated embrace. Constantine realizes the Christians now outnumber the pagans in the empire, and that the prudent thing to do is to get on their side. So in February of 313, Constantine issues the Edict of Milan. According to the edict, every Christian gets paid back double what the Empire has taken away, fifty new cathedrals are built, and, in short, Christianity now becomes law. Author Phyllis Tickle quips that in February of 2013 we should put black on every church door to mourn this fateful date, when Church and State became one. Power infiltrates the once power-less band of Jesus followers, and the church quickly becomes something unrecognizable to its former self.

Establishing the Empire as officially Christian increases unity in some ways, but Constantine quickly learns of infighting within the church. Some argue, from the Scriptures, that Jesus is divine, that he is a part of a three-person Trinity. Others argue, from the Scriptures, that Jesus came from God but is not to be equated with God. Not wanting such divisiveness, which was largely the point of establishing a state religion, Constantine convenes a church council to settle the matter in 325 AD. Yet before the Council of Nicea is even established, Constantine has already made up his mind: We are Trinitarian. He leads the council, reads the opening statement and gives the opening prayer. James Carroll, in his book, *Constantine's Sword,* comments on the results of the Council: "In response to the Emperor's mandate, the bishops did, in fact, agree to a formulaic statement of belief, defining especially, and in explicit terms, how Jesus is God. They did so unanimously—well, almost unanimously. Those who dissented were exiled by Constantine. Christians still recite this formula today, as the Nicene Creed."[1]

Basically, if you were part of the Council and didn't agree with Constantine, he destroyed your life, which would have been more than a little pressure to sign the statement of belief. (And I thought *we* took *our* theology seriously!) He certainly wasn't the sort of emperor you would have wanted to rub the wrong way. It hardly needs to be said, but it is really hard to imagine the Holy Spirit inspiring this sort of behavior.

Soon, Constantine decides he needs Bibles for all the new cathedrals he has built. He issues the command, and the question returns to him: "Umm, which books should be included?" You guessed it: Constantine decides which books. If you have a typical Protestant Bible on your shelf, you can thank Constantine for that. Constantine orders and finances fifty parchment copies of the new "Holy Scriptures." It seems with the financial element added to the picture, the Church fathers were able to overcome their differences and finally agree which books would stay and which would go. As one writer notes: "One can easily argue that the first Christian Bible was commissioned, paid for, inspected, and approved by a pagan emperor for church use. It would have undoubtedly been considered the canon of its time."

Not only was Constantine the Emperor, but he also understood himself to be the Vice-Regent of God. He exerts absolute authority over the church. The implementation of his strong desire for unity and control overrode any tolerance for diversity in both politics and religion. If people

---

1. Carroll, *Constantine's Sword,* p.189.

didn't affirm everything he said and did, they would be guilty of treason and, therefore, exiled or executed in all manner of unmentionable ways.

Constantine worshiped the Sun God (on Sunday) and believed that Jesus, the Son of God, was one and the same as his beloved Sun God, so he basically consolidated the two gods. Constantine didn't like Jews, and in the years that followed, he hardened some of the lines that had formed between the Jews and Christians. The severance between the two religions eventually led to extreme and horrendous treatment—which has carried throughout the history of the church—of anyone with even a hint of Jewishness on them. This attitude toward the Jewish people prevailed long into the future. Even our own Martin Luther despised the Jews, spewing words of hatred their way and encouraging the burning of synagogues. Beyond him, the repercussions of anti-Semitism have carried even farther, eventually to Hitler and his ovens.

With Constantine, a precedent has been set, and within a short 200 years, the Emperor Justinian makes it *illegal* not to be a Christian. The State and Church have become fused. In a sad, ironic twist of fate, the very empire that put Jesus to death now presides over his community.

As I continue reading and researching, our separation from the Jewish roots of our faith turns out to be one of the least disturbing bits of church history. As I dig more, I realize that the very basic, most obvious fundamentals of the Christian faith today were neither universally obvious, nor fundamental to the Christian faith until various councils gathered throughout history to determine them to be so. Tremendous diversity of thought could be found in the early Christian communities, especially regarding the nature of Jesus. A clear consensus regarding his divinity did not exist until Constantine laid down the law. This is news to me. I always assumed that our theology was exactly right, that even the disciples understood Jesus in the way I do. To discover otherwise troubles me greatly. It's unsettling, unhinging.

What's more, this diversity of thought seems to have been somewhat acceptable among believers. More important to the early Christian communities than unity of knowledge of the Divine, was unity in the way of life under the Divine. After all, who would claim to have complete knowledge of God and an absolutely thorough understanding of the nature of Jesus? Well, who else but the emperors who often considered *themselves* to be divine?

As the self-appointed Vice-Regent of God, Constantine put an end to the different beliefs about Jesus and essentially demanded that everyone must have a specific understanding of the nature of Christ. Constantine—*a pagan*—deciding for all the world who Jesus is?

I had grown up assuming that the Nicene Creed was spoken nearly word for word from the Holy Spirit to the writers. But it turns out that Constantine—with his threatening sword—spoke these "holy words." So my next question becomes: "Was Constantine the embodiment of the Holy Spirit?" It's hard to imagine the Holy Spirit in the form of a man who murders his own wife and mother, a man who barbarically commands his armies to slaughter many who refuse to embrace his way of thinking, a man with a great political interest in getting everyone in his empire to understand God in the same way that he did, a man who knows that if everyone sees God as he does then he can invoke the Divine in all his political causes and efforts (Wait. Something about this is all seems a little familiar). The answer seems to be an emphatic "No!" In fact, Constantine, in many ways, seemed completely contrary to an embodiment of the Holy Spirit, for that Spirit exhibits love, joy, peace, patience, kindness, goodness, faithfulness, gentleness, and self-control—which hardly bears any resemblance to the man Constantine.

But I find Constantine as just one example of so many people who act in such ways under the guise of faith. It turns out that church history is scattered with similarly corrupt Christian leaders who sought a plush life of power and influence. One doesn't have to look hard to find an abundance of scandal and mingling with corrupt politics woven in the ecumenical councils. These politically power hungry, corrupted individuals shaped many of our creeds and doctrines. Many selfish motives played into the shaping of the foundation of my theologies.

I am incapable of sleep. A restlessness claims me. I excuse myself frequently all hours of the day and night for long, unmapped, wandering, contemplative strolls down the streets of my neighborhood. *What sort of faith have I subscribed to exactly? Is this the foundation of what I believe? Something based on the ramblings of self-obsessed, power-hungry murderous, raging madmen?* I feel myself approaching a frightening madness as well. The ground drops out from beneath my feet. I find nothing firm to grab onto, no foundation to anchor me.

I continue reading through history's "contributions" to Christianity. In the case of Constantine, once he had his formula of belief for Christians in place and had secured his place as Vice-Regent of God, he strengthened the hierarchal structure of power within the church, designed after his empire. The early followers of Jesus, called "The Way," centered themselves on community—a way of doing life together, a way of being the communal hands and feet of Jesus in the various communities throughout the Empire. Despite the differing understandings of exactly who Jesus of Nazareth was, everyone agreed upon the mandate to care for the sick, feed the hungry, and clothe the naked. This was central to discipleship, the core of following Christ. These early church communities—in sharing everything, feeding the hungry, caring for the sick, and taking the homeless under their roofs left no one among them in need. However, it seems this hands-on discipleship model faded away when faith entered into a marriage with political power.

Though the church continued to perform great charitable efforts, such as setting up hospitals and caring for the poor, corruption in the church continued to expand and spread after Constantine. Controlling the people's specific religious beliefs with doctrines to which they were commanded to subscribe, acted as a great method for maintaining control of politics in the empire as well.

With the hierarchal structure in place, it became a simple task to make political decisions and pass them down the chain of religious command, deeming it "God-ordained." The emperor was the voice of God whispering in the Pope's ear. He passed on his decisions as the truth from God, which ensured support from the people, as no one could argue with God.

I came across Leo Tolstoy's book *The Kingdom of God is Within You*, in which Tolstoy points to the thoughts of the historian Helchitsky, who attributes the degeneration of Christianity to the times of Constantine. Tolstoy writes:

> Pope Sylvester admitted [Constantine] into the Christian Church with all his heathen morals and life. Constantine, in his turn, endowed the Pope with worldly riches and power. From that time forward these two ruling powers were constantly aiding one another to strive for nothing but outward glory. Divines and ecclesiastical dignitaries began to concern themselves only about subduing the whole world to their authority, incited men against one another to murder and plunder, and in creed and life reduced Christianity to a nullity.[2]

2. Tolstoy, *The Kingdom of God is Within You*, p.17.

Church fathers, such as Augustine, were not unaware of the tremendous scandalous nature of these church leaders—their own shortcomings notwithstanding. (We could write a whole additional chapter on Augustine's influence on theology, for better and for worse.) Yet figures like Augustine and others have been a steady thread woven throughout history, crying out for the church to focus more on the character of its power-hungry church leaders. Sadly, many of the individuals whom our corrupted church leaders deemed as heretics and burned at the stake were the pious ones whose warnings we perhaps ought to have heeded and whose examples we ought to have been following.

And so this all leaves me to wonder: *Did Constantine and the other corrupt emperors and church leaders that reigned during these critical times, when our creeds—the very foundation of how we understand the Text—were formed, get us off track from what a community of believers is supposed to be? Did they bind and gag the Good Shepherd, lock him in one of their dungeons or send him off with the others they exiled, then disguise themselves with a shepherd's staff-turned-cross and lead the flock down a path of submission to their own powers?* Certainly, it's these first steps off the path that are the most dangerous and the most critical because the first steps off the path are the steps that get us going in the wrong direction. And these seem no small steps, at that.

I wonder to myself if this marriage between the church and the empire slowly and subtly, throughout history, turned the focus of the Christian faith from the life of Jesus to the cross on which he died. From a place of focusing on embodying the *sacrificial love* of Jesus to an attitude that dwells on the *sacrifice* of Jesus.

I just can't help but wonder if we have lost sight of the Good Shepherd's staff, which leads us down his path and calls us to a way of life. Have we, over time, ditched the staff for the cross? Have we exclusively come to view the cross as a crutch, an excuse to avoid any self-sacrifice? A "He did it, so we don't have to" sort of philosophy? I frequently heard this kind of teaching in Sunday school as a child.

Over time, perhaps, we focused so much on the particulars of how we understand Jesus that we no longer focused much on the particulars of living like Jesus. And maybe those before us have even discouraged a Jesus-centered way of life. In focusing on living the way Jesus lived, there is a danger—we are told—that we might be distracted from the fact that we are saved by God's grace and begin thinking we are somehow saving ourselves.

Is the church today still driven by a politics of control? A top-down, power-brokered approach to theology, as in: "Believe this way or else"? Do we maintain a priority of grasping—and forcing people to sign on to—specific theological understandings over encouraging a way of life? Is it possible that there are pious men and women today, calling for a reformation within the church? Are they somewhere in the shadows, calling us to turn back to focusing more on the Text and living the life to which Jesus calls us? If there are bold individuals out there, speaking against the mainstream of Christianity, are they the men and women whom the church shuns, spits at, and casts aside as "heretics"? Am I one who sentences the Augustines of our day to the gallows? Am I on some side of evil—disguised as goodness—and completely unaware of being so?

As the dust begins to settle from my archaeological dig into church history, I feel compelled to share some of my findings in my Christian circles. Since I'm simply presenting the history I've stumbled upon, rather than expressing my personal concerns, I decide this is a safe way to get the discussions going. I want to know how other people process the information. Do they find it as disturbing as I do? Are they so secure in what they believe that the history behind it matters little? In nearly every instance of sharing, I get the same pat answer: "God has used all of history to bring us to himself. He turns the most evil moments of the past into fertile ground from which the seeds of truth and goodness sprout." Well, I easily recognize this answer because it's the same answer I was trained to give, unblinking and unthinking.

So what then is the goodness and truth that could have possibly come from the maddening spirit of Constantine, his armies, and the rest of the corrupt church leaders in our history? What is the gain of marrying the church to the empire? Is it that Christianity's alignment with power may have kept it alive? Is it our separation from, and superiority over, our Jewish roots and other religions? Is it the organized hierarchy of church structure? Is it the surrender to "absolute Truth," as imposed by the explicit creeds and doctrines composed within those hierarchal church structures? Is it the new and much easier focus on the cross as a means to get to the kingdom of God after death, versus a focus on following the shepherd staff down a sometimes difficult path in order to usher in the kingdom of God here and now?

Or, might the "unblinking and unthinking" answer be right? Is the ground still being tilled, still waiting, still making way for the seeds of truth to sprout and flourish from these grounds? Are there perhaps sprouts erupting here and there, scattered across the land, among the weeds and rocks?

I also have to consider the possibility that we might simply spout lines like this to justify the unjustifiable. We want easy answers to the evil within our own church history. We want to avoid the hard work of rethinking things, of measuring our doctrines against the actual words of the Text. Or maybe our pride and insistence on being absolutely correct in where we've arrived is the actual stumbling block that prevents us from peeling back and examining the layers of the history of these theological assumptions.

I can't imagine the Christian Reformed Church inviting a pagan murderer to step in like a king, declare himself to be the Vice-Regent of God, take over its top executive position, and enforce a completely new order. To be frank, I can't even imagine a person of non-Dutch descent being allowed to step into that position. But even this role in the CRC would be insignificant compared to the authority that men like Constantine were given over all of Christianity. The evidence suggests Constantine and those who followed in his footprints were often far more scandalous than murdering pagans. My denomination today would no doubt excommunicate any such madmen making such ludicrous claims. So shouldn't we, at the very least, take a somewhat critical look at what came out of these men and all the theology they handed down to us?

Where has the church gone since its early marriage to the empire? What about the church structures in place today? Or even the core of our Christian beliefs? Or the lifestyle of those who believe? Does the church today at all resemble the way of the early faith communities?

Throughout history, church structure generally held the same shape as the political structures of its time and place. For example, the church in America is more democratic. We have "congregational votes" to elect our leaders that resemble our national voting system—everyone gets a say because this is America, after all. Is this political philosophy justified for our church system? Something of authentic community and discipleship seems to get a bit lost within the various organized hierarchal structures of many churches today.

And then, again, that larger, more persistent question begins to afflict me: Where does the focus of my faith lie? In the *life* or in the *death* of Jesus? This is a scary question to me, and I tiptoe around it for a while. I can't take my eyes off the fact that the early Christians were all about embodying the life of Christ, living as he lived, *being* the living, breathing kingdom of God.

In time, the church shifted toward stressing proper theology—to knowing and understanding truth in a certain way—in order to enter that unimaginably wonderful kingdom of God that comes only after death. I suppose this is an easier umbrella to pull people under, to assemble the masses in order to better control them. "Simply subscribe to these statements of faith, and you will someday enter Eternal Paradise." Easy as pie. And in time, the way of life of believers began to mirror more of their culture and less of a Christ-centered community. The journey seems to have become more insignificant in light of the destination, the very opposite of what Jesus stressed. And eventually, like some box office promising The Show of the Century, you have the church literally selling tickets to heaven in the form of indulgences.

I am increasingly stressed. I'd like to go relax on the beach, with my head in the sand.

I have to ask these questions. I can't simply ignore the facts, though certainly ignorance would be bliss. But it's too late to turn back now. It's too late to wish I had never questioned things in the first place. I've ventured into one of those "dangerous" places. I have opened a door that should have remained shut. Yet I have to take a long, hard look at the past in order to move forward. I can no longer swallow my dark suspicions. The eyes remain incapable of erasing what has been seen in the history of the formation of my theological certainties. My brain is powerless to remove these stains from theology's whitewashed walls. A desperate need arises to work through these questions and inconsistencies. With no turning back, I step with two feet into this forbidden landscape. I dare myself to venture deeper into the bookshelves that have been off-limits, dangerous, even considered heretical. And yet, I tell myself, there should be no trepidation on this truth-seeking journey, for if it is indeed truth that I seek, then I must be willing to go wherever that path takes me.

CHAPTER ELEVEN

The Withering

BACK TO SQUARE ONE: *Why do I believe what I believe?*

In seventh grade, a bolt of doubt struck, and I raised the forbidden question in my Bible class: "How do we actually know that *any* of this is true?" It was extremely off topic, and an absolute silence fell over the class. After a moment of composure, my teacher seized the opportunity and assigned the class—everyone except me—to write a paper stating why the Bible is, in fact, true. The next day my classmates turned in their papers to me. My teacher then assigned me to review them and then explain to the class whose paper was the most convincing and why.

My peers jotted down a whole host of responses, none of them very convincing, and most of them quoting specific verses of Scripture as a defense of itself, which, when you think about it, makes no sense. Most had no idea except that their parents said it was so. Some papers were long and drawn out, but one in particular simply said, "There is nothing that can prove the truth of the Bible. You just have to have faith that it is the truth."

Faith. I liked it. I gave her a gold star sticker and decided just to have faith. It was that simple. I decided not to let that big question harass me anymore.

But now, as an adult, when I peel back the layers that surround that simplistic faith and begin to untie the theological strings that have tightly defined and bound it, that question boldly rears its head once again. I feel more and more disturbed, the more I uncover. Is it possible that we have gotten something even as basic as faith all wrong?

If the claim that Jesus is the only way to God is irrefutable, a known fact, then believing that claim doesn't require faith because it is already known. But since sufficiently complete evidence for the claim is lacking, believing it necessarily requires faith. But this also means that the claim that Jesus provides the only way to God is not a known, irrefutable fact.

What exactly is faith, anyway?

I actually have a life-long, well-rehearsed response to this question, straight from the Heidelberg Catechism and the list of answers I have committed to memory. If a CRCer can't say this one off the top of her head, word for word, one would have sufficient grounds to be suspicious of the authenticity of that golden certificate mounted on her wall.

> Q. What is true faith?

> A. True faith is
> not only a knowledge and conviction
> that everything God reveals in his Word is true;
> it is also a deep-rooted assurance,
> created in me by the Holy Spirit through the gospel,
> that, out of sheer grace earned for us by Christ,
> not only others, but I too,
> have had my sins forgiven,
> have been made forever right with God,
> and have been granted salvation.

The Catechism proved a wonderful way not only to supply the answers in my pot but also to control the very questions I was allowed to ask.

But a few European scholars created this definition of "faith" centuries ago. Notice its focus on knowledge and its bottom line of personal salvation. Today, we have abundantly more access to historical, cultural, linguistic information about the Bible than the writers of the Catechism. I feel compelled to do some research on this word "faith."

It turns out that "faith" is a verb, meaning it is an ongoing action one *actively performs*, not a one-time object one *passively receives*. I examine it in the context of Ephesians 2:8: "We are *saved* by grace through faith." Consider this word "saved." (We'll get back to faith in a moment.) The Greek word for "saved" in this verse is *sozo*. The word gets a bit lost in translation and resulting interpretations. The literal translation is closer to: "healed, restored." The word derives from the Greek word *saos*, which means "safe." Knowing the root of a word often helps us understand its meaning. In this case, "saved" means that through our active and ongoing faith (verb), we find restoration, healing, safety. Over the centuries, our theology evolved to turn the focus of salvation almost exclusively on eternity. When you read the word "saved," think more of holistic, complete healing.

The Western concept of faith places the action on the one in whom you have faith, such as "faith in God." In my tradition, faith is mainly an intellectual process in knowing that someone or something exists or will act. For instance, if I say "I have faith in God," I'm saying, "I know that God exists. I know he will do what he says he will do." Also, faith from the Western perspective almost solely links itself to eternity—the end goal. If you have faith in Jesus, you get into heaven. Period. End of story.

In contrast, the ancient Hebrew people had no concept of eternal life the way we now understand it. The Hebrew word for faith, *emunah,* means "support." In typical Hebrew fashion, a word's function defines it, and words often depict an action—what someone does. In defining faith, the Hebrew word *emunah* places the action on the one who "supports God." From this Hebraic perspective, faith is not knowing that God will act, but rather that *I* will do what *I* can to support God. Faith, then, carries with it the idea of "faithfulness."

Therefore, one does not have faith at a middle school church camp and get into heaven, but one continues to act in faith his or her whole life. To a Westerner, faith is about the end product (getting into heaven), whereas to the Hebrew, faith is all about the journey (living in faith daily). Jesus and the early Christians understood faith in this same way.

Again, how easily a word gets lost in translation. Salvation is not necessarily something to be solely grasped after death, as we Westerners often assume. Faith makes more sense to me in this light. The Hebrew background reveals what my faith compels me to *do*; whereas before, my faith was focused on what I should *know*.

So then, are our lives healed and restored by God's grace, through our faithfulness? What if this very practical, here-and-now wisdom better reflects the biblical model? Is it possible that the thing to be gained here is that if we live life in obedience to God, we will experience his grace with the gift of living more holistic, healthy lives now?

Let's reframe the biblical question: What must I do to be saved/restored/healed?

Many would say, "Believe in the Lord Jesus, and you will be saved/restored/healed."

Yet even the demons believe, and with a theology more accurate than our own, I dare say. But the demons are not saved, are not able to experience healing and restoration because they don't obey—they don't possess faithfulness.

Understanding "faith" as a verb also makes more sense considering the strong words of Jesus regarding the day-to-day way we live our lives. For example, the fruit of the Spirit is love, joy, peace, patience, kindness, goodness, faithfulness, gentleness and self-control. Jesus says that he who bears no fruit will be cut off and thrown into the fire. That is to say, he will no longer be part of the living, breathing kingdom of God. Regardless of what he believes in his head, his faith is not alive. Without faith, the fruit is nonexistent.

Perhaps in living out my faith, in living the way God originally intended for me to live, I experience healing, restoration, and wholeness. Could faith be that simple?

Faith is not faith without action. Or as James puts it: "Faith without deeds is dead." Faith is a verb. If I'm not faithful, then do I really have faith? Am I really healed/restored/saved? It seems that I can believe whatever I want, but my life will be hell on earth if my fruit reveals itself as hatred, sadness, conflict, impatience, jealousy, meanness, badness, faithlessness, harshness, and impulsiveness.

I can't help pondering the possibility that Jesus could be saying something like this: "Look, God created you. He knows the best, most holistically healthy way for you to live. And you can experience it here and now, if only you will be faithful to my ways. Come. Follow me." This understanding seems to point back towards a faith focused on the life of Jesus (the shepherd's staff) rather than on his death (the cross).

And so, while theology can be good and helpful, the better question is this: What am I DOING? It's good to wrestle with the Text, but where are my feet? Where are my hands? Jesus seems mostly unconcerned with my theology. He claims that if I don't care for the least of those among us, then I don't care for him. The weight of statements like this, from the one we claim to be God in the flesh, ought to weigh heavy on us.

So perhaps an important question I ought to be wrestling with is not "How do I shape my faith?" but "How does my faith shape me?" The best articulation of my faith to a devastated world will not be in the form of theological statements but in how I live my life. This seems to fall more in line with the Text.

≈ ≈ ≈

I have always assumed my faith to be true. But then, wouldn't people of all denominations say the same thing? Indeed, it is what many religions across the world claim. Perhaps plunging the depths of the Text to understand truth more fully is actually pointless. Is the Text itself even true? I don't know what to think anymore.

Certainly, for most of my life I believed what I believed because it's what my parents believe. My parents believe what they believe because it's what their parents believed. No doubt, if I had been pushed into the world from the womb of a Muslim woman in Iraq, I would be a Muslim, just as her parents were Muslim and her parents' parents. That would be the true faith, and all other faith perspectives would be wrong. If I ever questioned this, perhaps I would be told to "just have faith." Just because I've been told that a particular version of the truth is *the truth* doesn't necessarily make it so.

In his book *What Would Jesus Deconstruct*, John Caputo offers further insights on truth. He says, "On my accounting we are not preprogrammed or hardwired to the Truth (otherwise we would not be free) but proceed perforce by one form of faith or another, more often than not, the one in which we find ourselves. The reason we are on a journey, the reason we have our several faiths, the reason why the early Christians and Lao Tzu speak of following a "way," is precisely the contingency and givenness of the world in which we find ourselves and the desire we have for a guide."[1]

Nearly every Christian denomination makes a case that it is in sole possession of the truth. As a result, rather than continually searching for truth, we Christians often busy ourselves defending the "absolute Truth," which we claim to have indeed completely figured out. We have nothing new to learn, at least not outside of our theological boundaries.

This picture from Leo Tolstoy, in his book *The Kingdom of God is Within You*, speaks to this propensity in the church:

"Every church traces its creed through an uninterrupted transmission from Christ and the Apostles. And truly every Christian creed that has been derived from Christ must have come down to the present generation through a certain transmission. But that does not prove that it alone of all that has been transmitted, excluding the rest, can be the sole truth, admitting of no doubt. . . Every branch in a tree comes from the

1. Caputo, *What Would Jesus Deconstruct?* p.41.

root in unbroken connection; but the fact that each branch comes from the one root, does not prove at all that each branch was the only one. It is precisely the same with the church. . . A church is a body of men that claim for themselves that they are in complete and sole possession of the truth. And these bodies, having in course of time, aided by the support of the temporal authorities, developed into powerful institutions, have been the principle obstacles to the diffusion of a true comprehension of the teaching of Christ."[2]

Every branch of Christianity claims absolute truth, which, when looked at from a distance, seems absurd. It forces me to another consideration: Perhaps God works beyond our limited understanding, and perhaps each one of the different branches that stems from the same root, in some clandestine way, all lead to God. Surely, if there is a God out there, a God who fashioned the entire universe, he cannot be fully understood by human, rational capabilities specific to one specific time and culture.

If God can, in fact, be confined to the soil in my pot, then perhaps he is not God after all. For what kind of a God would be limited to human formulations? Do we ultimately design our own gods, deciding who God is and how he works? Are we made in God's image, or is he made in ours? Perhaps the rational minds of each particular time and culture merely order God in such a way that he can be easily grasped, understood, and even controlled. I wonder: *Does it come down to us fashioning God, rather than God fashioning us?*

I'm confused. Not sure what to make of any of it all anymore. I'm disturbed, actually. No, "disturbed" is an understatement. I'm incensed. I simply can't go on in this can't-see-straight, can't-sleep-at-night, can't-properly-digest-the-food-on-my-plate way anymore. Who can I trust? Who has the "right" version of the truth, or are they all right? Or are we all wrong? How could I have been so arrogant in my theological assumptions? How is it possible that my denomination actually believes that out of all the Scriptural interpretations ever made across the world, throughout history, we—here and now—got it all exactly right? All others are wrong, some forgivably so, and others not. It seems to me an absurd assumption, actually. There have clearly been some major, underhanded activities involved in and surrounding the formation of our theological understandings. But somehow, we have no problem ignoring all this history.

2. Tolstoy, *The Kingdom of God is Within You*, pp.54-55.

And this raises the question: *Do we actually care to know the truth, or do we primarily want to maintain the structures that have been built around our supposed truths, regardless of how ridiculous some of those truths become in light of the new biblical contextual evidences that time constantly unveils?*

No organized entity is without its politics. Is it possible that the church has evolved to the point of defending its particular theologies in order to maintain the structures built to house those specific understandings? Is there any room for the Text to breathe and move and speak to us in a new way today? Or has it all been figured out with finality? Can the Holy Spirit still teach us new things, but only within the theological lines we've drawn?

One thought leads to another, and another, and another. The questions start rolling in faster than I can manage them. It would have been nice if I'd have been encouraged to ask these sorts of questions over the course of my entire life because they now come racing in so fast that I feel overwhelmed, approaching paralysis. I wonder if there's a medication that can make me content with the status quo, shut down the activity in my head, stop the thinking, force some sort of seizure that makes my head nod up and down in agreement, remove all curiosity, make me forget all my questions. But then, of course, this wondering brings me to the realization that yes, there is a prescription that does all of that: it's called religion!

Fiddlesticks! Back to square one.

The fact that nearly all cultures throughout history have come up with some idea of a God to explain things now makes me wonder: *Are we simply created with a need to believe in a higher power and to organize that power in a way that makes sense to us?* With a belief in something larger than ourselves, religion fills in the gaps, explains what we can't understand, gives us a strong place to rest when weary, and provides rituals to practice these set beliefs. We find peace in knowing that no matter how many pickles life slings our way, we will be okay because our God is with us and will take those pickles and make amazing relish. Even the darkness of death can be explained away and is no longer a fearful thing, as God will transport us to an everlasting, all-inclusive tropical paradise. Pretty much all religions have some version of this same general story. That can't be coincidence.

~ ~ ~

I recall my brother Jon's terrible ski accident on the Colorado ski slopes, which turned his junior year in high school into a question mark as to whether he'd survive or not. Ski medics carried him off the mountain with a traumatic, closed-head injury. The first forty-eight hours after the accident were critical. He remained in a deep state of unconsciousness as Mom, Dad and I waited while a ventilator pumped artificial air into his lungs, sustaining his life. Tubes and wires flowed in and out of every opening in his body. It was frightful and unnatural to see my strong kid brother in such a fragile state. The doctors told us that if he were to wake up, we could expect that, at best, he would likely have severe disabilities.

I cried, shuddered, and collapsed. Shaken and hardly able to breathe, my tears became my prayers. I pled through my weeping. And that first night, despite all the chaos of life unfolding around me, a deep, deep unexpected warmth suddenly settled upon and within me, as if a blanket of love and goodness and peace had draped itself around my shaking shoulders, holding me and soothing me amidst the pain and uncertainty of what lay ahead. I could almost see a physical presence, could nearly grasp the silky edges of the blanket. I knew with certainty. I knew with certainty that whatever happened, the presence of God was with me. Whatever happened, I would be okay. I knew it. I felt it. I could see it. I have always attributed that warmth as God's direct response to my tears. And I often wondered throughout the ordeal: *How in the world would anyone get through tragedy like this without God?*

But now I wonder: *Was it all a psychological trick of the mind? Is God merely a panacea for weak minds? A nostrum for bridging the gaps in our logistically-ordered world?* The human psyche is extremely powerful and complicated. Had I experienced the warmth and comfort because my mind had been trained to expect such a response from an omnipresent God?

Certainly religion is healthy for people. It has worked well for me. It has truly strengthened me, helped me cope when all the earthly odds were stacked against me. It's like the frayed security blanket I've dragged all over the planet as a toddler and kept tucked under my pillow throughout my childhood. But is it true in the epistemological sense? Or in some other way? Or isn't it true at all? I'm no longer sure. I'm just no longer sure about any of it.

Perhaps it's all imagined. Perhaps in our longing to understand things we can't understand, we've created a God that we can somewhat understand—one that we can be in relationship with and trust. In this way, we can at least understand the one who understands what we are incapable of understanding. Maybe we find some measure of control and comfort in imagining a God. Yes, perhaps this is it. God is a figment of our imagination.

And so, after many months of back and forth debating within myself, I come to a conclusion. I choose to believe for all the benefits of doing so, even though I know the Christian faith isn't actually true. In fact, it can't possibly be true. Immediately, though, I discover that choosing to pretend to believe something I really don't doesn't sit well with me. In fact, it disquiets me and wears me down.

In all this pandemonium and agitation of my security, I begin to experience tremendous anxiety, the way I felt as a child when we visited some new place and my blankie was left at home, forgotten in some disheveled corner of my bed. I'm living in parallel worlds, a leader in a church whose community I love but whose theology I realize I no longer embrace. How can I go on existing in such a state of inner discord? I'm a living, breathing prevarication. A hypocrite, if there ever was one.

My inner turmoil becomes extreme, tears me up into a mound of slumpish fragments. I feel as if I'm being put through a slow-grinding paper shredder. Showing up at church on Sunday mornings becomes increasingly more difficult for me. "I'm not feeling well" serves as an easy excuse, and I use it several Sundays in a row.

Then there's family. I love my family. Parents. Siblings. I truly love them, and I can't imagine anything ever separating me from them. I'm terrified, panicked that they will reject me, cut me off, no longer love me for what I have become, for what I no longer am. I fear that they will feel completely disrespected and thoroughly rejected. It would be the most painful possible reality for them, the thing all Christian parents most hold their breaths against—hoping, praying that their child doesn't wander from the faith. And they will themselves be scorned, the subject of cruel gossip, somehow assumed to have failed in their parental covenant.

When I was a child, my mother used to hold me against her breast when I scraped a knee, pinched a finger in the door, or grieved the latest flattened kitty on the road. I don't remember my specific wound, but I have a memory of crying on her lap in this way, her arms wrapped lovingly around me, hand stroking my hair, and my ear pressed to her heart. I was entirely soothed, calmed by the sound of the blood rushing, pulsating through her ventricles. I sat until my heart fell into rhythm with hers. I can still close my eyes and hear it, feel it. This is one of the most comforting memories, and I mentally go back to that place even today when I need the presence of a calming thought. Now I find that aching desire to be physically present in that place, to again rest in her arms, to feel her heart beating against my ear, to pour out everything to her, and let all the pain melt away as she whispers melodies of love, comfort, and assurance in my ear.

But I'm unable to tell my family. I can't. And so I feel like a wailing baby ripped away from her mother's arms, desperate to be in them, but held back by the fear of exposing my painful truth and being tossed aside for it. Knowing that they will truly believe that their only daughter, and therefore probably their grandchildren as well, will one day die and spend an eternity in the flames of hell, leaves me scarcely able to breathe, even though I'm certain this idea of hell is not real. It kills me inside to know the depths of how this revelation will paralyze them, ruin them. Despite that, in reality, none of these things actually exist—in their world it is very real. All their anguish will be on my shoulders. They will take this pain to the grave, and it will disintegrate only as their bodies decay. And so unable to bear the thought of this, I decide I must instead take my secret to my death and continue the charade when around them.

One crisp, windy morning as the naked branches of the sugar maple scratch against the bedroom window, it all becomes too much to bear, and I break. Curled up in bed, unable to release my feet from the warmth of the down spread, no longer desiring to lift my head from the pillow, I start to cry. It's a sweeping release of all my inner disorder. I cry out the way my hungry babies wept when they were starved to suckle at my breast. The whimpering continues until my eyes swell shut and the hydration of my body empties itself, running from my tear ducts like an open spout, tears pooling on my pillow.

How long can I keep up this disingenuous pretense? Despite the benefits of belief, none of it is real. In fact, living in such extreme hypocrisy has, for me, erased any actual benefit that comes with the pretend belief in a higher power. How long can I maintain this false facade? How long?

There's no place for me. No place for a person who doesn't know what to believe anymore. Who will be my community? Where do people like me go? Bryan—having read and processed much of the same material—has been very patient and understanding with me throughout all this. At least I still have his hand to hold now that God is dead to me. I'll continue walking in the company of Bryan, of Bryan and Nietzsche.

Closet Homosexuality. I think I understand now. The heavy and painful burden of personal rejection as a means to survive in a world that is often cruel to the reality of who you are. I am a closet atheist. Part of me wants to pull my family away from this Christian town, away from our Christian families, to a place where I can be honest, guilt-free and authentic to who I am. Progressive Europe, maybe. "Let's move to Europe," I suggest to Bryan.

"Okay." He smiles, without glancing up from his book. I know we won't move to Europe.

Dumping the burden of my reality on those who love me will only result in a much higher degree of pain for everyone involved. Their pain will be the direct result of my personal convictions, so I will be doubly burdened. And so I have no choice but to continue bearing the burden of my pretending.

Deep depression sinks in. I've fallen into a dark pit of such great depth that I can't see even a peep of light when I look up, not even a tiny splinter of luminescence. The walls feel as if they're closing in. My chest tightens, and I strain to squeeze a sustainable amount of air into my panicky lungs. I must certainly be the only pastor's wife on the planet who has doubts about it all. Having a secret confined within the walls of our little bungalow creates a lonely existence for me.

My questioning despair inevitably leads me to ask: Is there, then, no purpose to the existence of humanity on this planet? Are we just another mammal who happens to be at the top of the food chain? Is the only real difference between a cow and me the fact that that I have a conscience and stand upright? Are we simply to live for a time, and then to die? From ashes to ashes, dust to dust?

I feel as if I'm walking around in a long, heavy, black, rain-soaked, wool winter coat that never dries. The buttons are stuck and I can't get it off. Or perhaps it's been cruelly sewn shut by some invisible hand.

I play Chopin repeatedly in these dark days. I'm seduced, hypnotized by the deeply satisfactory feeling of my fingers rolling up and down the minor keys of the piano. Chopin becomes my mourning ritual, like a melancholy funeral for the Lord God, who no longer is, who never was. God is dead. I scatter his ashes, and I wait. I wait for some great new hope to rise from this sullen reality. In the company of Chopin, I wait. With Nietzsche, I wait. Under dim house lights, I sit hunched over the black and white keys and allow the music to speak on my behalf. These spells at the piano generate terrible and beautiful moments for me. Salty and sweet. Detestable and desirable. Loathsome and longed for.

Waiting. Waiting for some new life grounded in my newfound Truth to rise up, to lift me from this darkness. I wait and wait, but a turning point never comes. God is dead, and his ashes have blown away.

Eventually, I pick up the guitar and dig deep inside, composing songs with unfettered honesty, from what bubbles and brews beneath my skin. I give voice to all that is awful and all that is beautiful in my soul. Complete transparency. Raw authenticity. Music speaks on my behalf, uttering note by note what I cannot express otherwise, releasing the broken pieces of myself. But the music reverberates, only to be absorbed by the walls with which I've surrounded myself.

Life begins to exist in a heavy, sticky atmosphere. I feel myself pulling away from people, convinced that someone will see straight through my exterior to the inside of me. Someone will become aware of the ugly lie I am living. The truth has a way of coming into the light. But I cannot reveal my truth, so I stay away from all those people with their shining little lights. Visits down to Holland to see family become less and less frequent. A variety of excuses keep me absent from church. I extract myself. I am an island.

My pot shatters, the soil seeps out onto the ground, and dries up under the heat of the midday sun, leaving my roots exposed and withered.

My faith is dead. I am dead. God is dead.

Chapter Twelve

Transplanted

FALL SURRENDERS TO WINTER. I no longer believe there is a God, and yet I believe it is good for people to believe there is a God. At its best, belief in God gives us purpose, creates community, comforts us, gives us hope, explains our origins. But because I no longer believe, for me all those benefits are absent. I keep my mouth shut, lest my inner thoughts escape and shatter someone else's illusion, drag them down into this pit with me.

Trying to grasp the origins of all things has become the one wrench, the one thorn in the side of my newfound atheism. For some time, I simply ignore it. It's as difficult to digest as a thick slice of great Aunt Frances' fruitcake. But as unresolved things usually go for me, I can't leave this lack of belief alone without some attempt at reconciling it. And so again, those cursed gears of my head start churning, keeping me awake at night with all their grinding racket.

Certainly I'm no scientist. In fact, every science class in high school—from biology to chemistry—kept my overall GPA in a humble place. And so as my small mind attempts to grasp big scientific concepts, I'm well aware of the possible holes in my way of thinking. But still, I allow my thoughts to run.

If there is no God, how did this whole thing get going? I wrestle through many nights, with my head in the stars, my eyes gazing out the window beside my bed, beyond and through the Milky Way, trying to imagine infinity going backwards. Did the universe simply always exist? Was there a time when there was nothing? If there was a time of nothingness, then how did the first something come into existence without a larger something to get it all started? Could there be a place for God in that process? Could he even be a *necessary* piece of the origins of the universe?

But if God put this whole universe into motion, has God existed for infinity? Infinity itself is simply incomprehensible to me. Infinity drives me crazy! I try to think back hundreds of millions of years, then trillions of billions of years, and we still haven't reached infinity. But then, suppose time didn't exist until the birth of the universe. Perhaps both time and infinity cannot be measured in increments of time. I find myself powerless to comprehend it all. And yet, *something* had to get the first thing going. It *had* to all come from *somewhere*.

But if it all came from God, then where would God have come from? Did he think himself into existence? Was the very first thing a clump of God's thoughts floating around in nothingness? I suppose if there has been something around for infinity, it makes more sense to my small mind that it would be some semblance of an immaterial being rather than simply a lump of matter. Perhaps some essence of God's thoughts willed himself into being, which then breathed the universe into existence.

Infinity circles my thoughts, unbroken for weeks. Eventually, in a great and deep exhalation, I begin to approach on tip-toe the possibility that perhaps there *is* some form of God out there. For weeks I weigh the possibility of matter spontaneously existing out of nothing, versus some greater force creating matter out of nothing. The thought of matter just appearing on its own seems incomprehensible. It seems highly likely that some sort of greater Being must exist.

The thought briefly runs through me that, perhaps, like a tortured individual at Guantanamo Bay, I am merely surrendering my thoughts and positions to the dominating thoughts of the community that surrounds me, as a result of pure mental and physical exhaustion. Too much thinking—resulting in sleepless nights and over-caffeination during the day—might have taken a toll on me, forcing me to give up my truth quest simply as a means of survival. But I brush these thoughts away fairly quickly as my puzzled mind wanders back to questions about origins, back to who or what caused the beginning of everything.

As the weeks wear on, I find new threads of hope as I notice the details and movements of the earth and my place on this delicate planet. I begin to think upon the possibility that God—whatever he or she is exactly— might exist. One morning I wake up from a restless slumber and find myself strongly embracing the internal suggestion that for this entire universe to exist, some God must also exist.

Maybe it's time to disrobe my atheism, I say to myself. To what end exactly, I'm not sure. I begin to speculate, with Isaac Newton, that perhaps God is like a clock worker, that maybe he sort of wound up the universe and let it go, come what may. Admitting the reality that God exists in no way bridges the great chasm that still lies between me and the specifics of the God of the Bible. I'm leaning towards Tolstoy's analogy of the tree— that several branches of truth come from one root. But unlike Tolstoy, the tree I envision has branches of Christianity, Buddhism, Islam, etc. The roots of my imagined tree, though, do not stem from the Jewish faith but rather from some vast, unspecific, incomprehensible being: unseen, unknown, and unknowable.

I continue dipping the bread in the wine, but its significance is some-what lost to me. I sing the songs of worship along with everyone else, but to me those songs are no longer God-specific.

Then one day, Bryan comes home from the pub, where he was hav-ing a beer with his friend, Mark. Mark had given him a book, *A New Kind Of Christian*, the first of a trilogy by Brian McLaren. The lamp on the nightstand stays on all night, and Bryan's vocal enthusiasm never desists. Right into the dawn, he carries on.

"This is your story! I can't believe the timing of finding this book!"

First thing in the morning, Bryan rushes to the bookstore in pursuit of McLaren's next two books, while I delve into the first book. Page after page, my eyes absorb the words as fast as they can. My soul begins to stir. It turns out that I am not alone in this after all.

The book recounts the intimate conversations between characters Pastor Dan Poole and a high school science teacher, Neil Oliver. The characters dialogue about faith, doubt, reason, and spiritual practice in the emerging postmodern world. I ingest the book. Can't put it down. De-spite being fiction, the ideas are obviously grounded in experience, and suddenly, I do not feel alone in my thoughts. Over the next couple days, I unflinchingly neglect my responsibilities and plow through all three books in McLaren's trilogy.

For me, this story arrives as a tale of hope and spiritual renewal, just as I thought I had lost the Christian God forever. McLaren presents a beautiful Christian faith in these stories, a faith that allows space for questions and error, a faith that focuses more on the journey than the destination. This kind of faith approaches biblical interpretation swathed in humility and exploration, rather than a spirit of already knowing it all before even cracking open the cover. McLaren's books introduce to me a Christian faith that expresses hospitality towards doubt. This open-ended approach to the Christian faith strongly resonates with me. And I wonder if it's possible that many like me have left the church, and ultimately God, because their church experiences held no space for doubt.

After chewing and digesting the trilogy, I order *A Generous Orthodoxy*, another McLaren book. To refer back to Tolstoy's analogy, if Christianity is like a tree with several differing branches sprouting unbroken from the same root, then McLaren reaches up, picks the best fruit from every branch and shares the feast. I find myself unable to turn my back on this irresistibly beautiful spread of food. I am starved for it. A luminescence streams in from somewhere above and drapes itself over the plump-ripe fruit. I sense a personal invitation to sit at this table and devour its goodness.

I feel drawn to the subtitle of *A Generous Orthodoxy*: "Why I am a missional, evangelical, post/protestant, liberal/conservative, mystical/poet, biblical, charismatic/contemplative, fundamentalist/calvinist, anabaptist/anglican, methodist, catholic, green, incarnational, depressed-yet-hopeful, emergent, unfinished Christian." With a healthy view of the Text in its original context as his measure, McLaren looks at the various expressions of Christianity, affirming that each denomination strives for a Christ-centered orthodoxy.

McLaren's thoughtful work comes to me as a fresh breath of air, a shaft of light slicing into my dark world. It's as if someone has lowered a ladder down into my pit of gloom, and all I need to do is slowly grasp the rungs and—step by step—make my way for the surface. I'll be back on steady ground. I contemplate the proposal that the Christian God is big enough to embrace us in our individual and various ways of worshiping and understanding him. Realizing that no one way could possibly have it all exactly right, I find a new sense of peace. I discover an unadulterated rest in the mystery of God, in the places of unknowing. Yet, I feel trepidation as I gaze up at this ladder. Do I trust it? Will it hold me? I've been on something similar before, and it buckled when I was at the top.

In *A Generous Orthodoxy*, McLaren points out some of the criticisms of my Reformed, Calvinist faith. Some devastating effects spawned from Calvinism, such as an overconfident certainty, and in that certainty,

Calvin went to the lengths to oversee the execution of fellow Christians who refused to submit completely to his system of beliefs. Later, when Calvinists came to settle in America, they used their certainties to steal land from the Native American population, as well as to justify the slavery of African peoples. In South Africa, Calvinists used such certainties to justify and defend apartheid.

McLaren also sheds light on the great contributions of the Reformed tradition, including some of the positive aspects of the character of John Calvin. McLaren quotes John Franke, formerly of Biblical Seminary:

> Reformed theology is always reforming according to the Word of God in order to bear witness to the eternal truth of the gospel in the context of an ever-changing world characterized by a variety of cultural settings: *theologia reformata et semper reformanda . . .* Accordingly, the process of reformation from the Reformed perspective is not, and never can be, something completed once and for all and appealed perpetually as the 'truly Reformed' position. In the words of Jürgen Moltmann, 'Reformation is not a one time act to which a confessionalist could appeal and upon whose events a traditionalist could rest.[1]

A truly reforming Christian never arrives at a point of absolute conclusion and settlement. Now I question whether my own tradition in the Christian Reformed Church is actually truly "Reformed," or whether there even is such a state. The word "Reformed" sits precariously in the past tense, as if it was once reformed and needs no further adjusting. But I don't think this is at all what John Calvin had in mind.

Calvin was brilliant and bold. He spoke up against the established Catholic Church, which meandered from the Text and equated every Catholic doctrinal/theological interpretation as biblical truth. Calvin created and offered his own intellectual theology to fellow disgruntled Catholics. At that time, one had to decide between being a Catholic or a non-Christian. Calvin offered an alternative.

McLaren raises a good question that all Calvinists ought to consider: "What would a brilliant, bold young Calvin do today, I wonder? Now we have a different problem. We have no shortage of establishments (including Reformed ones) and no shortage of lean and mean doctrinal systems.

---

1. McLaren, *A Generous Orthodoxy*, p.190.

Would a young Calvin today correctly identify a completely different need and boldly meet it with similar skill and passion? I believe he would."[2]

I'm beginning to like some things about this Calvin. *Who are the passionate Calvins today?* I wonder. *Who feels angered enough at the lack of reformation in today's church to do something about reforming it once again? Where are these Calvins today? Would the church even recognize them as such, or show them the door?*

As an introvert, long, silent, contemplative walks in the woods remain essential for me to maintain a healthy existence. One January morning, I head out for my daily walk to sift through the thoughts that have been stirring afresh in my mind and soul. Snow falls like white velvet, silently floating down, winnowing through the stark branches of the trees. I'm alone with the long early morning shadows. After climbing a strenuous incline on the trail, I sit on a bench in order to catch my breath, harness some peace, and absorb the stillness that lies all around me. As I settle in a clearing, perched on the top of a hill overlooking Traverse City and the Grand Traverse Bay, my exhausted hammering heart begins to quiet and my heavy, thickened breath slows and softens.

In my physical exhaustion, my thoughts and emotions coalesce with clarity. There is a hush in the air. Something esoteric happens within me; an ethereal swirling floats around and through me. Something resplendent and inexpressible. Weightlessness. Mental release. Letting go. New space, filled with something indescribable, permeates me. I can't exactly describe what transpires, but I know that it is good. I sense that it is of God; his whispering voice perhaps. He's calling me back.

The tears come. I am powerless to stop them. I baptize my dead Lord with the salty liquid that drips from my tear ducts and then pools over him. He breaks through the surface of the waters, cleansed and new, and wraps his arms around all the broken pieces of me, fusing them with his Divine love. The old God has died. The new has risen. He is renewed, no longer bound by my chains, but free. And in his freedom, I find my own. How good to be able to breathe again and to feel his breath on me, his light on my face. The warmth of his embrace runs through me the way a smooth glass of Pinot Noir slides warmly down my throat. The dark

2. McLaren, *A Generous Orthodoxy*, p.189

weightiness that overwhelmed me lifts. Falling from my shoulders, that heavy metaphorical coat pops open, and the drenched wool slides down in a heap beside me.

Through the crisp air, I descend the hill. I run back to the arms of Christ. Realizing that I can be a follower of Christ and be loved, even while harboring questions and doubts, arrives like a deep breath after a long underwater dive. A fresh excitement, a new passion to understand the Text swells with each step towards home.

Stepping through the door of a still-sleeping house, I shake the snow from my outer layers and peel off my mittens, boots and hat. While steaming water absorbs the flavor of the freshly ground coffee beans in the French press, I slide my Bible off the bookshelf and blow the dust away.

My roots, dormant and neglected, have been laying thirsty under the heat of the sun with barely a pulse of life left. Yet in this moment, they are picked up and transplanted into the damp coolness of the earth, amid the potsherds scattered all around.

I drink deeply.

Reevaluation. Reexamination. Measuring my life authentically against the Text. This is sure to be a lifelong process.

I find camaraderie with other Christian writers, as I settle in my big, brown leather chair, nursing my babies and sipping earthen mugs of Zen tea. After Brian McLaren come authors like Rob Bell, Phyllis Tickle, Marcus Borg, John Caputo, Peter Rollins, and others who unabashedly trudge the road less traveled. They plunge into the depths of the Text and walk wherever it takes them, regardless of how the larger established Christian community scrutinizes them. Many from conservative denominations quickly dismiss these writers without a fair trial—sometimes going so far as labeling them "heretics"—but I relate to them. They understand me and where I've been, like few I've come across in my faith tradition. They have walked this walk, wrestled the same historical and theological opponents, and passionately re-imagine the faith for today. Perhaps these are the John Calvins of today, the ones serious about the Text, humble in their approach, yet seeking to live and proclaim their faith in an authentic way.

Walking in step with these fellow transparent souls, I begin to breathe deeply, drinking in air and life again. Without them I would, no doubt, still be stuck in that no faith zone, would still be licking the salt of my tears in a room with the shades drawn.

Still, as comforting as it is to know there are others out there who harbor doubts while maintaining faith, as I do, I crave the physical presence of someone who understands. *Can I gather the courage to open up to one or two people, beyond my husband, about my doubts? What will happen? Will we no longer be welcome in our denomination?* I envision our house and health insurance evaporating because of me. The internal debate lengthens at approximately the same rate that my fingernails shorten, one of the great curses of my introverted nature.

When summer settles in, I give my friend a call. She's one of those rare people with a truly hospitable aura surrounding her. It's a warm evening, and we sit on the beach with a bottle of Shiraz to enjoy some honest conversation and a mid-summer sunset. After the usual chitchat about the daily grind of life, we progress to daring each other to follow our hopes and dreams, as we often do. A few moments of silence ensues, so as not to disturb the harmonious palate of a thousand colors erupting in the sky. The turquoise waters fade to deeper shades of azure, as our slice of the earth turns to face the moon. The colors of the sky smear together into eventual darkness, and we settle on our backs in the sand, gazing up at the stars.

The silence, umbrellaed by the divine dome above, invites my heart to unfold. This is as good a time as any. "I've been on this strange journey, and I'm not really sure exactly what I believe anymore." The increasing darkness eases the confession, with my face comfortably buried in the sunless atmosphere.

"What do you mean?" she asks.

Just enough wine has had its way with me, and I feel relaxed. "You know, God and all that. I just don't know about it anymore. I have some doubts about the way I've always understood him, the things that have been presented to me as fact. I'm just not sure. Everything used to be so black and white, but now most things seem to settle somewhere in various shades of gray."

She sits up, takes another swig from the bottle and turns to face me. "I can't believe this." She sighs and shakes her head.

Crap, I think to myself. *This is not the scenario I had hoped for.* I sit up beside her and stare out over the dark water, unable to face her.

From the corner of my eye comes the evidence that she's still shaking her head. "I just can't believe this." She starts laughing. It can't be the wine because between the two of us the bottle is only half empty.

I take the bottle and swallow a mouthful of confusion. I'm a tad annoyed by her reaction. "It's not really that funny, you know. It's been a hard road to walk. Anyways, never mind." I draw swirling patterns in the sand with the cork.

"No, no, no," she jumps in. "It's just that I've been struggling with doubt as well, for a long time. But whenever it surfaces, I just feel so inadequate, like a terrible Christian. I've been too terrified to discuss it with anyone, can't even tell my husband, so I just keep pushing it under all the time. I mean, who can you tell that you don't really know if you believe anymore, when all the people around you seem to have their faith perfectly together, seem to be perfect, unwavering believers? It's one thing to forgive and embrace sins, but who will embrace me in my unbelief? Turning to unbelief is like the epitome of evil."

I'm stunned. This is most unexpected.

She turns, looks me straight on and continues, "I just can't believe that I'm hearing it from a pastor's wife. It's like the first lady of the United States saying that she doesn't really believe in democracy!"

I laugh and parse my lips for another sip of wine. Shaking my head, I sigh. "I know. It's been awful! The past few months I've just felt sort of trapped in my existence, unable to express the truth of what is inside me. It comes with a disingenuousness that has plagued my soul. I've been so sure of everything for most of my life. So sure! But one crack, just one little crack, and it all started slipping out of my grip, like some great unstoppable avalanche. It just compounded and compounded, and before long I no longer knew which way was up and which way was down, and the whole thing came crashing down in a great heap of rubble."

"I just can't believe that I'm not the only one!" She cuts in again. "I really believed I was the only one! Oh man, you have no idea what I've been going through. This is just a huge load off!"

"Yeah," I said, "having been taught that every point of our theology was absolute and imperative to a true faith, when I uncovered one possible mistake among these theological assumptions, I wondered what else may be off. And this then led me to more questions. And then *those* questions led to the realization that it wasn't so easy to justify my definitive theology with scriptural answers."

I pause and reflect back to those simple days on the farm, when my faith was cemented to such certainties. "Perhaps if I had grown up holding a healthier understanding of Scripture while holding more loosely to theology, my path may have been different. In allowing room for uncertainty and mystery, a natural space opens and allows for inaccuracies and questions, without the immediate need to resolve them. If the whole package of theology must be absolutely one hundred percent accurate, then what are we left holding when one detail is obviously incorrect? The entire theological structure topples like a game of Jenga gone bad."

My friend and I share our stories well into the night, emptying our bottle of wine while filling up the star-lit skies with our questions and quandaries. I point her to some authors who have kept me company and helped make some sense out of the disruption of my faith. Now that we've established our bond of trust, I venture: "For me, God had to die in order to come alive in my life." I wait for her reaction. Those words floated around my head for so long but had not yet spilled onto the world's ears. Surprisingly, relief spreads across my friend's face, not repugnance. I explain how I've come to be on a new journey, seeking truth from the Text in its historical, geographical, cultural and linguistic context, without constant worry over whether my findings match up with a certain theological framework. I invite her to join me in this pursuit of the God who stretches beyond our theological articulations.

Soon after, I open up to another friend. Lo and behold, her response is similar! I can't believe it. I then decide to share a little of my story with a lovely small group of ladies from the church with whom I have coffee on Thursday mornings. Cautiously putting myself in a position of vulnerability, I start at the beginning of my story. A couple of the ladies began to speak up to the many ways in which they too resonate with my doubts. Later in the day, I receive an email from one of the other women who wasn't ready to speak to the group, but wanted me to know that she wasn't really sure about it all either. This particular group, for the most part, consists of a group of middle-aged women who grew up in the church—women planted in pots much like mine—pots filled with soil nearly identical to the dirt in my own pot, placed there by the very same hands. But as it turns out, many of us are unsure, while we pretend to be sure.

I come to realize that many others are externally pretending, carrying on with their childhood religion without completely believing in it—holding onto it for the purpose of acceptance and belonging. This raises another question: *What about all the people who grew up in church communities but left as adults?* I speculate: *In the process, I'm sure many have left not only the church but God as well.* This church evacuation seems to be a growing trend in my denomination and elsewhere. Church leaders across the globe ask the same question: "What can we do to keep the young adults in our church?" I wonder if one reason why young adults might leave their faith and church is that they simply need room for their doubts. They, like me, need to be allowed to ask any question, to explore outside the confines of their traditional theologies. And sometimes, the answer we need to give them must simply be: "I don't know."

Word spreads, as it tends to do in small faith communities. Soon, people come out of the woodwork, expressing their own doubts and wondering how to handle them. Rather than working to swallow these doubts, to push them beneath a false facade, or to remind each other to "just believe" (knowing they will be continually regurgitated while leaving a bitter taste behind), I often say, "Embrace your doubts."

I tell people who come to me to talk about their troubled faith to put their doubts to work. To allow them to fuel a passion for studying and understanding the Text on a deeper level. In my case, doubt was a necessary fertilizer for my growth. I no longer believe simply because someone has handed me something "I should believe," but because I've wrestled with it and worked through it—on my own and in community with others.

Watershed begins to draw in people who have been raised in the church, but for a variety of reasons, left it, and in some cases, abandoned God as well. People start trickling into our church with stories strikingly similar in tone to mine. The stories draw from the same book of many chapters, outlining the different forces that coerced these young adults to abandon their childhood faith. After years of attending Sunday school classes and church services, after a lifetime of memorizing and regurgitating the specifics of a neat, well-packaged God, these wayfarers woke up one day and realized they never really understood *why* they believe as they do.

Like me, no one had encouraged these friends to ever explore the Text in a deep, genuine way. They adopted the faith of their parents, but most had never claimed faith as their own in an unfeigned, bona-fide way. And because they hadn't taken ownership of their faith, it had no real impact on the way they lived. The result: such a powerless faith easily slipped away.

As we exchanged our stories, a common motif emerged: many churches we'd experienced seemed to emphasize believing the right doctrines while failing to actually follow Jesus in the real world. The whole point of church seemed to be "getting people into heaven" with little relevance in this world. The church is then charged with hypocrisy: failing to *actually* follow the person they *claim* to follow. But in reality, it isn't hypocrisy so much as a mistaken emphasis: caring more about upholding *doctrinal statements* about Jesus over *living* in such a way that makes a statement about Jesus.

As I consider how to nurture healthy roots in my faith life, my thoughts drift back to my parents' flower farm, where I transplanted thousands of flowers. If the roots became unhealthy or damaged in the process, the plant would either die or emerge stunted and weak. The healthier and deeper the roots, the more beautiful the blossoms that eventually unfolded. But if the roots were unhealthy, even a small gust of wind blew away the shriveled seedling on the surface, like some desert tumbleweed.

Perhaps the same can be said of faith. Doesn't Jesus say that by our fruits he shall recognize us? Not by our words or by the correctness of our theological comprehensions, but by our fruits. With so many young people leaving the church, I wonder if it has anything to do with being surrounded by a lifetime of indoctrination, with little benefit of tasting the fruit. Who would want that? Who would be excited to transplant a crop that yields little? People need to have deep convictions about a way of living if they are to flourish as healthy believers in new and different settings. Otherwise, even a slight wind might send them tumbling across the lone, dry desert.

In a nod to our beginnings on the beach, our church meets outside under a grove of trees all summer long. One particularly warm Sunday, early in June, a couple shows up and asks me: "Is this the church we've heard about? Where people can come if they don't have everything figured out, where it's okay to have more questions than answers?" Nodding in confirmation, I explain that we study the text in-depth and in community, with the goal of knowing Jesus in his context and living like him in ours. I also add that we don't claim to have all the answers, and aren't even sure if that's a goal we should have. Our purpose, in line with the early disciples, is to live in the hope of the resurrection, to lay down our lives for a broken world.

Another woman from Watershed begins meeting with me for coffee. Having grown up in a typically conservative evangelical church and family, she'd begun silently to harbor doubts in college, and ever since she hasn't believed in Christianity—at least not the version passed on to her. At some point, she decided to simply focus on the life of Jesus and found solace in caring for neighbors and for the earth, which included recycling and purchasing organic and fair trade products. "My faith came alive again," she shared, "but my parents got angry." They expressed disappointment and labeled her a liberal. They thought her rediscovered faith was a passing phase. She silently wept, unable to catch her tears before they dripped into her latte. "I love my parents," she sputtered, "but I can't reconcile their remarks that I'm on a slippery slope to hell." And she hadn't even spoken to them of her actual theological doubts! She had simply sought to follow Jesus in the daily, mundane grind of things. To her parents, however, these practical changes smelled of political liberalism. In their minds, this meant the devil had gotten hold of their daughter. Unsurprisingly, she wanted to run from this understanding of faith.

Like so many others, she also spoke of her extreme gratitude at finding a faith community where she could be honest and vulnerable, where she could worship a God larger than anyone could contain in a narrow theological formula. Here is a place, she noted, where all are welcome regardless of where they happened to be on the spectrum of Christian belief. "Where else does a church like this exist?" she asked. "Nowhere that I have ever experienced." We wondered together how many others are out there, silently suffering, playing the pretending game, having no place to be real.

As I exit the café, I consider how many of us have experienced superficial levels of Christian community, in which we unwittingly reduce God to the shallow soils of our containers. I muse: *How can Christians fully grow when their roots are bumping up against the bottom of the pots in which they've been planted?*

CHAPTER THIRTEEN

Foreign Soil

A STRANGER CAME TO my church one day, slid into the pew a bit after the janitor had pulled and released the thick rope that set the church bell swinging back and forth, gathering the speed and sway to clang loudly overhead. I'll never forget that Sunday, so long ago. I must have been five or six years old.

This stranger in our midst surely felt out of place in his worn blue jeans, weathered plaid shirt, unshaven face, and disheveled head of hair—an eyesore amid a conglomeration of shiny people sitting in the polished wooden pews. Heads turned. Children, myself included, strained to position ourselves and unashamedly stare at this sad mess of a man. We gawked with our mouths wide open. I'm sure I'd never seen someone in this state before. So far did my jaw fall that Mr. VanderKolken could have driven his shiny black Cadillac up my bottom lip and right down the hatch.

A foreigner in our midst. He scarcely moved his lips when we sang songs from the blue Psalter hymnal. Confusedly flipping through pages in the Bible during nearly the entire message, the stranger had no idea where to find the referenced passage. He apparently realized how pathetic he looked and how misplaced he was because he disappeared in a flash as soon as the pastor said, "Amen." Whisperings filled our church over this unexpected event. Many experienced it as a complete disruption, but to me, nothing this exciting had happened at church since little Ronnie VanderMeulen dropped a blue Psalter hymnal from the balcony during the opening worship song, and it came crashing down on Mr. Scholte's head, knocking his toupee off center and rendering him momentarily unconscious.

The stranger never returned. No doubt he couldn't afford the necessary attire for our weekly "Sunday best" worship event. Or perhaps he deemed his life too messy to meet the bar of our sparkling holiness standards. Regardless, he provided us a new topic for our speculative gossiping during the post-service fellowship time as the adults sipped their coffee and us kids sucked down the typical sugary orange drink. No one ever mentioned the stranger again, as if we should not concern ourselves with his plight. We could not rearrange our tidy lives for his, certainly.

On another Sunday, when I was a bit older, we headed to church as usual. But this day, as we wound our way past farmhouses and freshly mowed alfalfa fields in our wood-grained station wagon, we saw a man staggering along the road, like a hung-over drunkard. He wore ripped blue jeans and a long underwear shirt, yellowed in the armpits. As we pulled up closer, we saw blood smeared on his face, his hands, and all down the front of himself. Dad instinctively pulled off the road. My eyes grew as big as saucers. I could barely believe this was *my* life, not some Hollywood movie scene.

Dad asked the staggering man if he was alright. The man's words tumbled out, his downcast eyes avoiding contact, "Yeah, I'll be fine." Then Dad did the unthinkable: he offered to drive this strange stranger to his destination. I thought, *This man has probably just murdered someone! If we pick him up, he'll probably pull a knife on us too!* Then terror struck my mind: *What if he squeezes in the back seat next to me?* Repulsed now: *He's gonna' get blood on my favorite Sunday dress.* It turns out that the gory-looking man declined. He thanked my dad for the offer and shuffled off, as if heading nowhere in particular. And my dad slowly pulled away. He didn't say a word, as if this is usual Sunday business. I was too stunned, too confused, too relieved to even say a thing.

Years later, this encounter still leaves an imprint on my mind. His bloodstained shirt and swaying walk, his head cast down and his hidden eyes haunt me for years to come—but not the bloody part, nor the drunken part, but the part where he refuses to get into our station wagon full of our family dressed in our Sunday best. Something else shocked me too: my Dad extending hospitality to a stranger, at the unknown risk to his family.

John Caputo talks about this kind of hospitality in his book *What Would Jesus Deconstruct*: "There is always risk in everything worthwhile. We are always put at risk whenever we welcome someone, just as we are put at risk whenever we love or trust or believe in someone, and the greater the love or hospitality, the greater the risk."[1]

What am I willing to risk?

Hiking our way down the hilly terrain of ancient Philadelphia, Turkey, we approach the outskirts of the modern city. We are a group of fifty dingy, dusty travelers, aliens in the land, speaking an unknown language. On the heels of my former teacher, we walk the same paths as the Apostle Paul, learning and absorbing. Bryan and I are excited to be here, having left the kids—now four, with little sister Josephine on the scene—in the care of family and friends. Side-by-side we study the early church in its historical and cultural context.

The town mosque blares the call to prayer on our approach. The eerie Arabic yodeling comes as a sharp reminder that we are in a culture that has long since given up its Christian and pagan religions for Islam. It's the last day of Ramadan. Muslims everywhere prepare food for the final celebratory feast at sundown, after a month-long period of daily fasting.

Approaching the city, we come upon a smattering of small dwellings connected by stonewalled courtyards. Ribbons of smoke waft up from behind these ancient partitions. Our group tramples down a narrow street as if we own it, looking left and right at the dwellings in this Turkish village. Here we walk ancient stone paths, untouched by time. It is easy to imagine that we might actually bump into a soldier from the Ottoman Empire, a sword-wielding Crusader, or even a hooded monk on his way back to the monastery. Yet the occasional Fiat sedan spouting smoke and the frequent satellite dish piping in MTV serve as jarring reminders that we have not, in fact, traveled back in time. One hiker from our group pokes his head into a small courtyard, assuming the open gate means that he's welcomed. Like nosey gawkers who can't help but slow down to look at an accident on the freeway—one by one people from our group peer in. I wonder what they see.

I grab Bryan's hand, not knowing if we should follow suit. *Is this rude?* I wonder. He gently pulls me with him, and we peer into the private courtyard, noticing a Muslim woman in traditional Turkish garb bent over a small fire. A gentle smile emerges, inviting me to take a closer look.

1. Caputo, *What Would Jesus Deconstruct?* p.77.

I notice her long, worn skirt spread upon the dusty floor of her makeshift kitchen, her head wrapped in a traditionally colored scarf. She squats on the ground before a convex pan over a fire, baking fresh bread, looking as if she's been doing this all her life.

A young boy wearing tattered pants, possibly the woman's grandson, approaches us. I assume he'll slam the gate shut in our faces. Instead, he tenderly motions with his arms for us to stop. A waifish young woman, perhaps his mother, or maybe his sister, follows with a large serving platter of steaming flat bread. She holds it out to us, and after hesitating, our group consumes each piece, clearing the plate. She briefly disappears and returns with another full plate. Despite the approaching feast to celebrate the end of their month-long fast, the matriarch has determined to happily sacrifice her family's bread to a group of well-fed Americans.

Stunned, we slowly savor the bread, our smiles reflecting gratitude. Yet as I taste this delicious home-made goodness, I recall my dad's act of radical hospitality. Again the question: *What am I willing to risk?* plays in my head like a spinning top stuck in a corner.

I try to imagine the converse scene: *What would the response in a typical suburban American neighborhood if a group of fifty Muslims came marching through, peering into our fenced-in yards?* Probably the constant fear-based narrative, reinforced by the popular media, would take effect: *All Muslims are terrorists. Call Home-Land Security! Code Orange! They are not to be trusted. Flee immediately! Hide your children! Save yourselves!*

Yet here in Turkey, a Middle-Eastern Muslim country, these so-called "scary and dangerous" people welcome and honor our group with unparalleled hospitality. Their immediate, unrestrained hospitality puts me to shame. This family has been fasting for a month, and as they prepare for the feast that ends their fasting period, they give their food away to complete strangers. As I recall our various media and military campaigns against the Middle East, I begin to wonder: *Who, actually, are the scary and dangerous ones?*

This exceedingly generous hospitality grips me, shaking my shoulders. Something unexplainably simple and pure washes over and through me. I realize that I have seen the face of Jesus, have tasted his bread fresh off the fire. Jesus, a veiled Muslim woman. Something catches in my throat, a lump that I simply cannot swallow.

Tears slip down my sun-parched cheeks, hang for a moment, then finally drip down, splashing on the dry dirt road beneath my feet, sending up micro-mushroom clouds of dust with each pitter-patter. I find my legs cannot move, as if glued to this spot. The entire group suddenly comes to a standstill. On this road in Philadelphia, we collectively come to a stop, and a great, invisible wave washes over us all, an aura of deep spiritual essence descends upon us. Our hearts and minds coagulate, suddenly harmoniously cognizant of the fact that something really beautiful has just taken place. A moment of stillness is needed for us to absorb and memorize the exact moment when God showed up to teach us a thing or two about love.

I feel myself gazing into a mirror, taking a hard look at some reflection of myself. I see myself side-by-side with the Muslim family we've just encountered. *Would I be viewed—by an outside observer—as being as much of a disciple of Jesus as this Muslim family was to me? Do people of other faiths have something to teach me about Jesus? Can these soils outside of my former pot also nourish me?*

Theological concerns dissipate, becoming pale when compared to the living display of love and hospitality demonstrated so beautifully by this Muslim family. The desperate quest of so many to have all things pertaining to God so neatly organized and confined within tight theological structures seems ridiculously paltry in comparison. Each step of this trip draws me into a deeper embrace with the Divine, but this moment tops them all.

In the moments of clarity and resplendence that lay in the wake of the encounter, I realize with an inexplicable clarity how my pot has restricted God's ability to work in my life. I see how the soil of my religious upbringing has stunted my personal growth and has limited my experiences. True rootedness in God comes from being planted in the open soil, not from living life in an exclusive, protected enclosure.

The pot can be a beautiful thing when the seedling is young and tender. A certain amount of nourishment and protection greatly benefits the seed as it first begins to germinate and slowly push down roots, as plump little sprouts first burst through the soil. But unless the seedling is transplanted, the roots will eventually curl in on themselves, choke each other out, and the plant will be stunted. The confines of the pot limit growth.

Simply put, my pot had become an obstacle in my attempt to embrace discipleship fully. In my meager attempts to define God, I had suffocated him. For too long I confined him to the limited terminologies of language and circumscribed intellectual capabilities. "This is exactly how God is," I would say, "and this is exactly how he works." But what if he chooses to work in some other way? Would I have failed to recognize him, ignored his voice or, heaven forbid, passed his voice off as the voice of the devil?

This is not to say, of course, that we should follow every voice that beckons us—far from it. But shouldn't we leave the door of possibility open for God to speak outside of the ways we predetermined him to speak? Shouldn't we allow him to work beyond the boundaries we have assigned him to move? Shouldn't we always be on the lookout for him and realize that he may even have something powerful to teach us from people of other faiths? The truth is, I may well find him in the soil *wherever* I trod.

In the moments that follow this encounter, I sense my roots spreading wider and deeper. I let go of the remainder of my need to control God. I say goodbye to my need to define and contain such magnificence in my inadequate, humanly ordered theologies. The mourning I experienced over the breaking of my pot now turns to dancing.

I am finally free to be transplanted into the world. My roots are now unshackled and able to stretch themselves deep into the earth, to push down through the soils of *all* of creation. I will grow tall and strong and beautiful. I will provide shade for those who are weary and fruit for those starved for it. My branches will sway with the breezes passing over, pointing ever to my Maker.

After receiving the shared bread, all the effort of juggling and getting straight the specific theological nuances of God seems entirely petty. An incredible peace and an ability to rest in all the unknowns of God falls over me. Rather than shouldering the burden of understanding him and carrying him around with me everywhere, this newfound freedom allows him to carry me. As my roots explore and expand into the unfamiliar soils of the earth, I find groundedness in him.

I let go of God, finally freeing him completely from his cage, allowing him to live and breathe and move and have his being in any way he must. He is free to have his being in the fullness of ways only known completely to himself—perhaps, or probably, outside the bounds of our traditional theologies. God is far bigger than my understandings can grasp. He cannot be summarized in the pages of some theological discourse, shoved in the backpack of a seminarian. He is not known more by the student who aces the systematic theology course than the student who skims by with a *D+* in a basic Bible class. He is not more real to the one who has memorized every question and answer of the Heidelberg Catechism, or more exact to the one who can recite the Nicene Creed forwards, backwards and in five different languages. While theology and doctrine can be helpful tools when kept in proper perspective, they are not the substance of true faith.

It seems that Jesus' life, death and resurrection have power in the lives of those who have encountered faith in real and tangible ways. I was shown such power in the face of a Muslim woman who—motivated by her own faith—demonstrated love in the simple act of extending sacrificial hospitality to a group of foreigners in her midst.

My heart, my life is now truly open to his Spirit, which blows like the wind. And because he may move in new and unexpected ways, I am now always on the lookout for him, eager to encounter him, excited to study the text in order to live it. The Word of God is again alive—it has jumped off the page. My faith is renewed.

The pieces of my pot are an important part of the history of my tree, its tall branches, its fruit. Bits of that first soil still cling to and provide nourishment for my roots, even as they push through new soils and gather new strength. And so while I still embrace some general foundational truths of my early faith, I now hold more loosely to my *definitions* of God and more tightly to the *ways* of God. The old adage "Actions speak louder than words" proves true. As a disciple of Jesus, the way I live ought to be a picture of who God is, an imperfect but ongoing work of art. I may be the only picture of God a person ever sees.

I want to survey those in my life and ask them: "What do I look like? What sort of God do I project out into the world?" And again I recall familiar words from the Text: "By their fruits you will recognize them." Love, joy, peace, patience, kindness, goodness, gentleness, faithfulness, self-control. *What fruit is evident in me?* I wonder.

Theology often places the focus of its faith on the fact that Christ bore the cross so I don't have to. I get that. In my sinful state, I am incapable of shouldering the burden in the flawless way he did. And yet Jesus himself says, "Take up your cross and follow me." How do I reconcile the two?

We tend to equate "carrying our crosses" with the avoidance of certain behaviors—drinking, drugs, sexual promiscuity, swearing, stealing, and so on—as if pain and sacrifice come exclusively from avoiding certain behaviors. But it seems that the people Jesus gets upset at—those he reserves his most harsh words for—are not those who break these cultural moral taboos, but the ones who claim to be his disciples yet turn their backs on the least among them. Perhaps the burden of carrying our crosses involves the sacrifices that come with being *proactive* followers of Jesus.

As a hopelessly flawed individual, I recognize my dependence on God's grace for experiencing wholeness of life. But as disciple of Jesus, I must at least strive to walk his walk, to love the unlovable, to show kindness to my enemies, to pray for those who persecute me, to feed the hungry, to clothe the naked, to give a cup of cool water to those who thirst. Not simply because God asks these actions of me, but because if I am truly a disciple, then my abundant love for him *longs* to live this way.

I should want to be so in step with Jesus that the dust of his sandals kicks up over me. While my humanity is often a stumbling block, the movement of my feet will be very telling. If I really am a disciple of Christ, then I should see within myself a desire to follow him passionately, despite my imperfect execution.

We can easily pat ourselves on the back for attaining a Puritan lifestyle, but what about when we fail to embody the very thing we are called to *do* as image bearers of Christ? Avoiding walking like Jesus doesn't provide an interesting topic of gossip like someone who's been caught smoking pot in the back alley. Perhaps we choose to busy ourselves by focusing on the "sin" of certain behaviors in order to avoid staring at the obvious reality of our own basic failings as Jesus' disciples. When someone sacrifices something in order to take in the homeless, for example, or sells their stuff to help supply someone else's needs, we call that exceptional person a "saint." But aren't we all called to live such lives? Shouldn't this be the norm for all of us who claim to be disciples of Christ?

Jesus focused on justice and love, and instructs his followers to do the same. Jesus calls believers to love the very ones they hate, to be a brother to those who hate them. Is it any wonder that crowds were drawn to this man Jesus? Who wouldn't be drawn to a beautiful love like that? Jesus didn't stand on the street corner and rattle off the five points of T.U.L.I.P. or spout out doctrinal creeds. He embodied a love that embraced those deemed by all the world as unworthy of love. He preached a radically new, subversive message that we love our enemies, pray for those who persecute us. He lived—in so many ways—completely contrary to the messages of his own culture, and certainly to our individualistic popular culture today. In contrast, many—even from our pulpits—tell us that we deserve bigger, better and more for ourselves, that we have a right to inflict revenge on our enemies, that the poor deserve to be poor. Would Jesus even recognize himself in his followers today?

In high school I spent a summer in California participating in a program that trained me for doing the work of evangelism. We learned and memorized a basic presentation of the gospel and then headed out, knocking on doors to shovel Jesus into strangers' living rooms. If I managed to avoid having the door slammed in my face, the next step was to outline the way to "get saved," hope the individual would say yes to the plan, and then pray a prayer of acceptance with them. Then I'd close with, "Here's a church brochure. Come if you want. Good-bye, and have a nice life." It all sounded so good, so clean-cut and easy.

Evangelism. I was good at it—very persuasive with my rhetorical skills.

Now, in the wake of this powerful encounter with Muslim hospitality, I'm discovering that perhaps the key to evangelism is genuine hospitality, rather than a polished presentation. In receiving their hospitality, I felt myself wanting to run to their open arms, to be part of their beautiful communal existence. I think back again to the day the stranger came to visit us at church and I wonder. I wonder what genuine hospitality would have looked like in that scenario.

Typically, I plan out hospitality like an event. I set a date, invite people over, clean the house and remind my children to be on their best behavior. Nothing wrong with this kind of hospitality. I can bless my invited guests. But what about the unplanned event of this stranger showing up in our pews? What if someone had invited him over for dinner on the fly, despite inconveniences, even with an unplanned meal and a messy house? What if we had been wearing something other than our Sunday best that morning, creating a more approachable, less-perfect, less-intimidating physical space? What if the stranger overheard not the typical—"Hi, how are you?" "Good." "Good."—but people sharing their honest, personal struggles? What if our hospitality extended even beyond opening up our messy homes to opening up the messiness of our lives?

Perhaps the stranger would have come to realize and experience the truth that we really are all as broken as he, and he too would share his brokenness and come to know and experience the love of God, rather than simply hearing about it. Perhaps he would have found himself enfolded into the kingdom of God, drinking deeply of God's healing grace and forgiveness. Perhaps this stranger in the pew would have realized that we all have a desperate need to be real. Perhaps restoration would have begun.

We may have been the only Jesus he ever encountered, and what a depressing experience we must have been.

In our faith communities, are we willing to go beyond traditional hospitality and be hospitable with our very lives? Are we willing to stop pretending we're saints and reveal our flawed and sinful selves? Are we willing to admit that we don't have all the answers and that perhaps we aren't even supposed to?

What about me? I ask myself a litany of questions: *Am I willing to open my door immediately to let strangers into my home and into my heart? Am I willing to put a hold on my schedule, to expose my messy house in order to embrace the stranger within my gates? Will I display a love so deeply with my arms wide open to even the most pathetic, unlovable people of this world?*

What am I willing to risk?

Now that I have experienced the deep and beautiful open arms of God on the streets of ancient Philadelphia, I find myself with a deep desire to share it not simply by telling the story but by embodying it to the world I find myself in. I have never experienced goodness, generosity—*hospitality*—in the powerful way this Muslim family demonstrated. They simply smiled and gave what they had.

Finding God in the soil of the Middle East. *Who could have imagined?*

Chapter Fourteen

Broken Branches

I CONFESS, THERE IS much to love about belonging to a particular denomination. Growing up in such a community, I held a certain security in knowing that specific underlying assumptions of belief were inherent in every individual. We could disagree as to whether or not the sanctuary carpet should be blue or beige, whether the pews should be cushioned for more comfort or remain solid wood to maintain a posture of alertness. It was acceptable to raise the question as to whether a person could legitimately worship God in blue jeans or if formal attire ought to be required, or whether the pastor should be allowed to remove his suit jacket as long as his tie remained securely in place.

But there was never a doubt about who was saved, never a question about the ways of God, no lack of conviction that God wanted the elephant's hoof to kick the ass come November. A uniformity of belief, framed and understood exactly the same by everyone. An umbrella of unity over us all. And truly, this measure of security gave us comfort, and more than that, it gave us confidence.

Yet, in my experience, this confidence had a hard time containing itself and nearly always bled over into arrogance. Not only were we exactly right about everything, but all others outside of our little sorority of specific and narrow pledges were wrong. We were God's elect, predestined for an eternity with him, but those who weren't us could never be sure where they would spend eternity, and we never felt held back from pointing out this fact. During much of my life, I assumed that when Jesus said, "Narrow is the path that leads to life," he was being prophetic, referring to the Christian Reformed Church that would sprout in North America in the 1850's and finally get it all right. It was another underlying assumed truth.

In one sense, we can see our theologies as the glue that binds us together and defines our community space. But I wonder if, in the broader scope of Christianity, our theological certainty sometimes divides us. When confined to the bubble of our little subculture, bound by specific and divisive beliefs, we can develop a smug air of superiority, acting like we belong to some elite spiritual upper-class. Are we sometimes like the popular crowd in junior high who walks around in a tight pack, noses in the air, sneering at those not dressed in trendy name-brand clothes? It saddens me when I see Christians using their various theologies to war against each other. This environment can be a ripe breeding ground for arrogance, for attacking the wrongness of the other, and defending our own rightness.

I grew up with a very specific understanding of God, as did most others in their various subcultures. Many have been born, raised, married, and given birth to the next generation—all without ever leaving or giving much consideration to the world outside of their subculture. Many view the world in an uncomplicated, black-and-white sort of way. They know for certain what is right and what is wrong. They know for certain who is going to enjoy heaven and who will burn in hell. Because they are so banded with like-minded individuals, it becomes easy to huddle together and point out the rightness and the wrongness of everyone else. It becomes easy to demonize and judge the other while exulting the righteousness of their own ways.

When I left my subculture and headed out into the world, I experienced culture shock. I got to know personally those whom I had demonized for much of my life. As I stepped out of my bubble and into many others over the course of my life, I've realized that—just like me—others are also products of the processes of socialization within their communities, with worldviews akin to their particular culture. In many cases, over the course of their lives, they had learned to demonize people like me, as well. I learned that these are not evil or bad people. They too strive for spiritual truth with the theological tools they've been handed. More and more, the complete black and whiteness of my former understandings blend into various shades of gray.

As my faith changes along the journey, it becomes increasingly difficult for those in my former subculture to understand me. Regardless of the fact that I'm on a deep quest to understand the biblical text, to seek seriously the way and truth of God, to take discipleship more seriously than I ever have before—I've increasingly become a target of demonization because this quest sometimes takes me down a different path than I formerly would have ever considered. This doesn't always sit well with Christians on the main road.

Of course, I must resist the urge to demonize them as well. I have to continually remind myself that they, too, are products of socialization within a specific subculture. Their own experiences no doubt vary to some degree from mine, so we'll see some things differently. We'll walk different theological paths. And having once held tightly to their general worldview, I especially need to understand, to extend grace.

That said, I don't think having theological assumptions is a bad thing. Our seeds need to be planted somewhere, and so we all come from a particular place of understanding. We all cling to those worldviews—theological, political and otherwise—with various degrees of certainty. However, I see it as quite damaging to demonize the one who sees the world through a different lens from our own.

Too often, we focus on pointing out the flawed theological particulars of the other and the rightness of our own, and don't spend enough energy simply trying to embody Christ. We stare so much at the cross—arguing over what it means—that we forget to pay attention to the path that brought him there.

A friend of mine once asked a Jewish rabbi why the Jewish people refuse to accept Jesus as the Messiah when all biblical evidence points to him. The rabbi soberly replied:

> A Jewish person looks at the rabbi's disciples to understand their rabbi. Just look at Jesus' disciples today. Look how severely fractured they are, constantly fighting over who is right and who is wrong, spewing words of condemnation at those who disagree with their theologies. Christians seem more concerned with defending their rightness than caring for the least of those among us. They say they have faith, and yet they live no differently from the world around them. Jesus lived a radically different life focused on unity, sacrificial love for the unlovable and justice. Jesus can't possibly have been the Messiah because he holds absolutely no power over the hearts of his disciples.

Ouch!

Christians are supposed to be disciples who follow Christ. And as such, we ought to strive to live as he lived. Theology is always going to be an endless dispute. But in one's practice we can see where one's faith actually lies. Whereas theology is the warm-up exercise, ethics is the real event. Jesus is more interested in our human interactions, in how we treat each other. The way we live our lives reveals to the world what we believe.

Often, when Jesus speaks of something akin to hell, he refers to those who tout knowledge of God in their minds but whose feet remain inactive—those who can rattle off some attributes of God yet don't seek to embody those attributes. These folks, Jesus claims, will not inherit the kingdom of God. In fact, they who bear no good fruit will be cut off and thrown into the fire, according to Matthew 3:10.

Or take the sheep and the goats, for example. In Matthew 25 Jesus talks about separating the sheep from the goats, which I always somewhat simplistically understood to be a separation from those who *believe* the right things from those who don't. As I read on in Matthew 25, I realize Jesus speaks of a separation between those who respond to the pleas of the least of those among us—those who *act* on his behalf—and those who ignore their cries.

Concerning the sheep he says, "The King will say to those on his right, 'Come, you who are blessed by my Father; take your inheritance, the kingdom prepared for you since the creation of the world. For I was hungry and you gave me something to eat, I was thirsty and you gave me something to drink, I was a stranger and you invited me in, I needed clothes and you clothed me, I was sick and you looked after me, I was in prison and you came to visit me.'"

Later, he addresses the goats: "Depart from me, you who are cursed into the eternal fire prepared for the devil and his angels. For I was hungry and you gave me nothing to eat, I was thirsty and you gave me nothing to drink, I was a stranger and you did not invite me in, I needed clothes and you did not clothe me, I was sick and in prison and you did not look after me."

Do I hear these words? If Jesus is God in the flesh, then Jesus' exhortation to care for those in need ought to weight heavy on me. Statements like this leave little room for theological disagreements. If the primary focus of Christians could become *living* faith, if we could be unified in embodying the sacrificial love of Christ, I am convinced the whole world would want to be part of it. We would truly experience the kingdom of God.

But if we huddle in our exclusive circles, and the tie that binds us is a particular set of knowledge claims that we have determined to be absolute, we remain powerless to effect change in the world. When I make it my business to draw lines, build walls, determine who is in and who is out, and judge who has faith and who doesn't rather than focus on my own faithfulness while leaving the judging part up to God, I become a weak witness to the world. The power of the life, death, and resurrection of Jesus is reduced to a nullity.

The events of history have twisted the focus of the faith from orthopraxy (right practice) to orthodoxy (right belief), and an enormous partition has risen between us and other believers. Clearly, God is unknowable in the absolute way we all, in our various Christian sects, think we precisely know him. If he were so obviously able to be—and intended to be—confined to a specific set of doctrines, and if that was the primary concern of Christianity, then wouldn't the Text have outlined it all with definitive clarity?

Jesus, however, is very clear about the way in which we must live, if we are his disciples. Even our theology affirms that God came down and slipped into human skin—shouldn't we pay attention to the way this incarnated God lived? If Christians would focus more on that and less on the theological particulars, we'd see much more unity in the larger scope of Christianity, and perhaps our walls would even begin to dissolve.

Today, it seems that when each denomination speaks about Jesus, it's actually speaking about itself. It then projects itself out on the world, leaving those in the world standing around scratching their heads, confused, wondering which version of Jesus to believe, as each one claims the pure version of him. Author John Caputo speaks of this denominational hijacking of Jesus: "The name of 'Jesus' is too often a mirror in which we beholden our own image, and it has always been easy to spot the sliver in the eye of the other and miss the two-by-four in our own."[1]

Each strand of Christianity decides what Jesus looks like, and then molds him to fit their truth. But shouldn't we seek the actual truth of Jesus and allow his truth to mold us? Are we so hung up on maintaining the structures and specifics of the truths within our various denominations that we render ourselves incapable of imagining that Jesus could possibly have some deeper truth to teach us—outside of, or different from, that

---

1. Caputo, p.34.

which we are already certain? Or that perhaps a much larger umbrella of truth encompasses all of us in our diversity of thought?

All this denominational division must be confusing for the world around us. All denominations claiming to be exactly right—it doesn't take a genius to step back and see the absurdity in this. We ought to approach God with far more humility than we do, it seems to me. If Christians across denominations would focus less on their particular theological refinements and more on embodying Jesus, I think we would find that we might actually all be walking the same path. The world might even begin to listen to us if we stop talking so much with our mouths and start speaking instead with our hands and feet. Perhaps simply the example of Jesus—loving God and neighbor—would tear down the walls that divide us.

Sometimes our theologies, though temporarily binding, can be divisive in the larger sweep of things. Jesus was well aware of this possibility. Consider his final prayer in the garden before he was arrested. He had just prayed for his disciples and now continues with this prayer for all believers:

> I pray also for those who believe in me through their message, that all of them may be one, Father, just as you are in me and I am in you. May they also be in us so that the world may believe that you have sent me. I have given them the glory that you gave me, that they may be one as we are one: I in them and you in me. May they be brought to complete unity to let the world know that you sent me and have loved them even as you have loved me (John 17:20–23).

In addition to praying for unity among believers, Jesus closes his prayer with this final plea: "Righteous Father, though the world does not know you, I know you, and they know that you have sent me. I have made you known to them, and will continue to make you known in order that the love you have for me may be in them and that I myself may be in them" (John 17:25–26).

Jesus isn't making a plea that his followers be clear about the breakdown of the Trinity or the fine points of predestination. Rather, his prayer for believers is that we experience God's love, become filled with it, and in the same way make it known to the world.

Knowing someone is not the same as knowing *about* someone. Really knowing a person requires an encounter, an experience—while knowing about something requires little more than a search on *Wikipedia*.

When I discovered I was pregnant with my first child, I read numerous books on pregnancy and the birthing process. I was pretty sure I had become an expert on the whole childbirth thing. I knew all about it. But when my belly began to bulge, when I experienced the baby's movements within me, when my breasts began to swell and ache, when those first incomprehensible moments of labor began sending wave after wave of seemingly unending excruciating pain rippling through me, when my body felt as if it were being torn open as my Henry came screaming into the world, when I first held his sticky body in my arms and tears of pure and absolute love ran over him erasing all the pain of the previous moments, I quickly realized that none of those books had adequately prepared me for reality. Now I understood pregnancy and giving birth. *This* was knowing. Only in the experience had I truly come to know.

Isn't the same also true of God? I can learn all about him from a particular assumed-to-be-true theological perspective without ever really knowing him. Imagine if the world came to *know* God through actual encounters with him? What if instead of judging those we find most despicable, we wrapped our arms around them and left the judging up to God? What if we showed the world how to live life in the Spirit rather than simply telling them? What if we actually loved our enemies rather than talked about loving our enemies while pursuing revenge? What if issues of poverty and the American healthcare conundrum dissipated because all Christians took Jesus' command seriously to care for the sick and feed the hungry?

Is it possible? Would Christians ever be willing to tear down these fortified walls and come together in community, to lay aside theological differences and embody the essence of Jesus in a world so desperate for him? In the least, it does seem perfectly possible to hold our differing theologies without constantly pointing out the rightness of our own and the wrongness of all the others. To be bound together in various communities of faith while entirely respecting those who believe differently. To recognize that we are all seeking truth, have all landed with our differing strands of truth through the various historical and cultural influences we ourselves have encountered, and to cling to them humbly.

"By their fruits you will know them." What would our world look like if Christians focused solely on ushering in the kingdom of God? What if orthodoxy took a back seat to orthopraxy?

When I think about unity in the body of Christ, I wonder if in some larger sense, it's possible that one denomination is a hand, one is a foot, another the mouth. Maybe our differing ways of understanding God are helpful—maybe even necessary—because they speak in a language familiar to those various subcultures. It might even be beneficial for Christian communities to have to their own theologies, to have a unity of understanding within each community, as long as we claim those understandings humbly, admit our limited knowledge and not cast stones of judgment on those communities of faith whose understandings differ from our own.

When our theologies cause unkind division within Christianity, when we toss grenades over our walls and into the compound beside us, we damage the body of Christ. Imagine the hand shooting a cannon at the foot, the elbow piercing the lips with poison, the stomach slashing the heart, or the arm forcing daggers into the eyes. Self-mutilation. It's a sad witness to the world, completely contrary to the essence of God, which we seek and claim to embody. And it should come as no surprise that the world often runs from us. And it should be no shock when young people, longing for an authentic faith, flee the church in droves.

What have we done to the resurrected body of Christ? What have we done? Have we forgotten that it is *we* who are the resurrected body of Christ? What have we done? A dismembered body holds little or no power in a world that is desperately grasping for wholeness.

Indeed, a body such as this might just as well be shoved back in the tomb.

CHAPTER FIFTEEN

Inconclusive

ONE STEP AT A time I walk.

As I walk on new ground, treading new soil, my roots continue to push deeper in the earth, to spread, and stretch, and grow. They reach through the dirt, grasping at the diverse nutrients a vast landscape offers. The whole world has become my pot. The deeper my roots, the stronger my branches. The longer and stronger my branches, the more fruit they offer to a world hungry for it, and the more shade they provide for those who seek a place of respite. The less I worry about defining and defending God, the more I seem to encounter him. I do not despise the pot I was given, I simply outgrew it.

Some readers might have pressing questions for me to answer. In the end, however, the answer is that sometimes I simply don't have an answer. I continue to be in process. In prayer, I find that I am often called to be the answer to my own prayer. In conversations, I am freed from having to "get it right." In moments of pain, I simply seek to be present. In the face of deep mysteries, I am comfortable letting the questions linger. When overwhelmed, I trust the larger purpose. At the end of the day, I seek to play my part in the larger whole.

Now, if my life collides with an individual suffering through difficult times, I no longer feel the need to dig through the limited soils of my pot for the correct answer. I don't try to make something up. Chances are, a verbal response will be insufficient. Love is the answer. To wrap my arms around them. To be present. To cry with them when they are broken, feed them when they are hungry, clothe them when they are naked, provide shelter if they have no place to lay their head, celebrate when they celebrate, and mourn when they mourn.

Love, the greatest commandment, serves as my guide. I express my love for God in the way I love others—especially those the world refuses to love. Love trumps the law. Love is bigger than the constraints of our various pots, which it turns out, must break if love is to flow through them. Love is not confined to a single religion or single approach to religion. Love is found in the very essence of creation—*in its very soil*—because as someone somewhere once said, "God is love."

In the end, faith turns out to be fairly simple after all. But it is far from easy.

Questions for Discussion

Chapter 1

1. How has your upbringing shaped you? What factors in your early environment stand out to you? What are things you cherish? What things do you wish might have been different?

2. The author had a close family, as she relates her story. Is your family close? Why or why not? What determines whether a family is "close"?

3. Are we shaped more by nature or by nurture? How much do our parents shape us? Our genetic makeup?

4. Discuss what aspects of faith and religion your parents or grandparents taught you, either implicitly or explicitly.

Chapter 2

1. Describe the fear the author experienced as a fifteen-year-old standing before the elders of her church. Does this resonate with any experiences you've had? How does your church allow people to become full members?

2. Did your family mandate church attendance when you were younger? Is there a better approach to encouraging family worship?

3. The author describes the observance of the Sabbath (Sundays) when she was a child. Did you have a similar experience? How do you think about Sabbath now?

4. As you read about the denominational differences between the CRC and the RCA, do they make sense to you? Would these differences

still be divisive today? What other issues seem to be more pressing for churches now?

5. Were certain books deemed "dangerous" in your tradition? Why might we label certain books or authors that way? Is that valid?

6. Discuss the difference the author experienced in worship at a youth convention as opposed to her experience in her home church. How have you experienced differing worship styles? What is most meaningful to you in worship? Does God mandate a specific style of worship?

7. Describe the author's desire to preach. Have you ever desired something that was deemed off-limits? Can or should women preach?

8. The author describes a close tie between her religious beliefs and her political outlook. Do your religious beliefs impact your political perspectives? Should they?

9. Discuss the author's understanding of evangelism. Do you agree with it? What is evangelism? How have you experienced it?

Chapter 3

1. The author notes that: "Where I come from, all Republicans are *not* necessarily Christians, but all Christians *are* necessarily Republicans." Describe the relation between faith and politics where you come from.

2. Discuss the air of self-importance that the author notes is ever-present in Washington DC. Does this surprise you? Is there any way for this to be different? Is there a line between pride and self-importance?

3. Does the description of street conditions in the nation's capital surprise you? Are there homeless people where you live? What is the responsibility of a community towards its most marginal members?

4. Is the approach of ignoring the needy in person while trying to help them "through legislation" a good one? What other approaches might be considered? Do we do the same thing when we send money to a cause versus going and helping in a hands-on way?

Chapter 4

1. How might traveling to Israel help you better understand the Bible? Have you done this? Do you know someone who has? If one is unable to afford or make such a trip, are there good alternatives?

2. Have you ever had to rethink your understanding of a biblical passage? What are the best ways to understand a particular text of Scripture?

3. Has the author's experience shifted the way you read Psalm 23? How do we normally think about "green pastures"? How might we think about them in light of the geographical context in which this Psalm was written?

4. Does the "American Dream" fit the biblical picture of the life of faith? How has "stuff" taken an inordinate place in the life of the average American Christian? What steps can we take to seek simplicity and dependence on God?

5. Discuss the rabbi–disciple relationship. Is this the picture you've had of what it means to be a disciple of Jesus? Since we can't physically follow Jesus around Galilee, what does it look like for us to follow him where we live now?

6. Have you ever asked God to make a certain situation easier? Do we do this perhaps too often? What does it mean to pray for "feet for the journey?"

7. Discuss the difference between waiting for God to act and stepping while the picture is unclear. Why is the latter so difficult? Where might God be calling you to take a step of faith?

Chapter 5

1. Describe the author's method of sharing her new faith insights by displaying rocks on her desk. Do you like this method? Have you ever done anything similar? How do we balance waiting for spiritual conversations to happen versus initiating them?

2. Is the National Prayer Breakfast proof that we are a Christian country? Should leaders from other religions be given a more prominent

place at this event? Should they be excluded? Does this event violate the separation of Church and State?

3. Discuss the author's description of President Clinton, and Democrats generally, as being baby-killers. Is this a useful description? How is such an attitude fostered? Can you relate to this extreme dislike of a particular political party? Is there a way to move beyond this attitude to a more helpful engagement?

4. Describe the interactions with the men from "The Family" and C-Street. Does this seem like a legitimate organization? How do you know when people are being honest, or are using spirituality as a guise for a different agenda? Was the author right to run from the mansion?

5. Discuss the author's experience at the State of the Union address. Have you ever been wowed in the presence of somebody famous? What is it about a celebrity that causes us to forget all her foibles and place her on a pedestal?

Chapter 6

1. Are people homeless because they are lazy? What other factors might be in play?

2. Look up the definition of *phronesis*. How is understanding the context important in understanding what the right thing to do is in a given situation? Is it possible to have hard and fast rules that *always* apply? Or does *phronesis* mandate otherwise?

3. The author notes that "the system often creates the very problems it later shakes its fist at." What is she describing? Do you agree? If so, what can be done about it?

4. Discuss the Grassroots Jesus Plan. Do you like it? How does hands-on service affect us differently than writing a check or helping from afar? What are the limits to such an approach?

5. Have you ever experienced an evening like the author's date with William—a time where someone let you down and showed you his or her true colors? Did it rupture the relationship?

6. Have you ever helped someone like this drunken Vietnam veteran?

Why do we usually "pass by on the other side"?

7. Describe the author's bold encounter with a fellow Republican staffer. What led to her eruption? Have you ever wished you spoke up like this but remained silent? When is the appropriate time to "give someone a piece of our mind"? Do you agree with her rant?

8. The author says flatly, "If Jesus were here today, he would not be a Republican." Do you agree? Why or why not?

Chapter 7

1. How much time do you spend reading or studying the Bible as compared to reading other books, watching television, listening to the radio? Are we influenced more by things we spend more time with?

2. Are you ever puzzled or confused by something you read? Does it make you want to read more or less? Are there things we shouldn't read?

3. What could we learn from the practice of "sitting *Shiva*"?

4. Do you ever feel alone? Do you ever feel you can't say what you really think? How should we handle such situations?

5. Have you ever felt genuinely conflicted about what was the morally right thing to do? Can these conflicts be resolved? Should they be?

6. Is there tension between the beliefs and actions of your political community and those of your religious community? Should there be?

Chapter 8

1. What was your first impression of the church-planting strategy? Do you know what strategies were used to start your own home church? Has the "playbook" changed?

2. The author asks in frustration, "Must it always be about the numbers?" Do we impose our own values on others with the questions we ask? How can we show a genuine interest in others' projects without projecting our own goals onto them?

3. Have you ever decided finally to turn something over to God? What happened?

4. Do you think God answered a prayer that Sunday when over twenty people came to church? How can we tell whether a special event is an answer to prayer?

5. What do you think about Watershed's approach to "structured church programs"? What are the advantages having or avoiding them?

6. Is there a proper balance between drawing people in and sending people out? Which do we need to work on most? How can we do that?

Chapter 9

1. Have you ever felt your conscience pricked by the actions of another person? What does that feel like? How did you react?

2. Is it possible to live an ordinary middle-class life *and* be a committed follower of Jesus? Why do so many of us resign ourselves to the former? What, if anything, needs to change?

3. What does Jesus mean by 'take up your cross'? What do you think the author means when she's asking whether she has taken up her cross? Do we take up our crosses?

4. Is Plantinga right when he says, "What we do with our time and resources, reveals everything about where our loyalties lie."? Where do our loyalties lie? How would things look different in our lives if our loyalties lay entirely with Jesus?

5. Are we more concerned with our bodily health than with our moral or spiritual health? Have you ever submitted to or given yourself a thorough moral check-up? What tests would you run? What do you think you need to work on most?

6. Do you think of your shopping habits as either revealing or expressing your faith? What should a follower of Jesus take into account at the store?

7. What should we do about governments, corporations, or systems in

general that function by exploiting people? Do we have a responsibility to avoid them? Repair them? Fight them? What specific steps could we take?

8. How can we talk seriously about contentious issues like the relation between politics and religion with people we know will disagree with us? Is there a way to make such a discussion respectful and productive?

Chapter 10

1. Are you curious about the origins of your religious beliefs? What could we learn by better understanding these origins?

2. Did the diversity of thought among even what most contemporary Christians consider to be fundamental surprise you? What might that tell us about Jesus' disciples, or Jesus himself, or the accounts of him in our Bible?

3. Should Constantine's spiritual fruitlessness influence our attitude toward the Nicene Creed? How would you react if a more contemporary tyrant were to try to enforce a common creed?

4. Is there any value to enforcing assent to a common creed? Is there any value to encouraging diversity of religious thought? What's more important?

5. Constantine claimed to be God's Vice-Regent and claimed to speak for God. Should we be skeptical of a leader who claims to speak for God? Do we all speak for God in some way? How can we tell whether someone is actually speaking for God?

6. Does God use unbelievers or downright evil people to accomplish his ends? Is there any way to know whether God's ends were accomplished in a particular situation?

7. "Where have we gone from Constantine? What about the church structures that are in place today? Or even the core of our Christian beliefs? Or the lifestyle of those who believe? Does the church today more closely resemble the way of the early faith communities or are we closer to the way of Constantine? And where ought we to be?"

8. What do you think of the author's reasoning in the following passage?

"[I]f it is indeed truth I seek, then there must be a willingness to go wherever that path takes me in order to find it. ... [I]f I indeed hold the truth, then it should stand up solidly against whatever I uncover."

9. Do you remember when you first had a serious religious question or doubt? What did you do in that situation?

10. Is the idea of being "saved by grace through faith" something you've affirmed? Did you understand what you were affirming? Has your understanding of this passage changed?

11. How can we "support God" or be more faithful? What can we do to bring restoration and healing to our relationships and our communities?

Chapter 11

1. What influence has your birthplace and environment had on your religious beliefs? Would you be a Christian today if you had been born into a Muslim, Hindu, or Buddhist family? Does that suggest a change in our attitudes toward people of other faiths?

2. Why does the author suggest that "Just have faith" is an inadequate answer to our deepest religious questions? Do you agree?

3. Do you agree with Caputo, when he says, "I maintain that no one really *knows* the way, not in any deep-down epistemologically unshakeable way"? What could you say in defense of your knowledge that someone of a different faith couldn't?

4. What do you think of Tolstoy's tree analogy? Is God too "big," too complex for us to understand? If not, what does that say about God? If so, does it make sense to express certainty in the truth of theological doctrines?

5. Do we know what God is like, or have we imposed our own ideas on God? If you had grown up without learning any theology, what would you think God was like based on your own experiences?

6. "[D]o we *actually* care to know the Truth, or do we primarily want to maintain the structures that have been built around our supposed truths?"

7. Why does the author say, "It would have been nice if I'd have been encouraged to ask these sorts of questions over the course of my entire life"? Do you think that would be a good idea?

8. Have you ever wished you could unlearn something you learned, or ignore your deepest, most troublesome questions? Would that be a good thing to be able to do? Does religion sometimes function that way for us?

9. Can you think of a time where belief in God was a source of comfort? What would you have done without that belief? Is belief in God a "panacea for weak minds"?

10. Do you understand what the author was going through, the tension between her doubts and her role in her church? Do you know anyone else who has been in such a situation?

11. Would you know if members of your church or your own family were going through theological turmoil? What is it about our churches and families that makes those who question and doubt feel so alone? How can we best respond to those we love who are struggling and suffering in this way?

12. What was the author's insight into our LGBT friends, family and fellow congregants who stay in the closet?

13. What do you do when you're depressed and feeling alone? What would you do if you couldn't turn to God, family, or friends for help?

Chapter 12

1. We often think of atheists as hostile to believers, so what do you make of the author's concern for her Christians friends ("I keep my mouth shut, lest my inner thoughts escape and shatter someone else's illusion, drag them down into this pit with me.")? Do you have any friends who have become atheists? Does the author give you some insight into their feelings?

2. How would you answer the following questions the author wrestles with, and what reasons could you offer to defend your answers? "If there is no God, how did this whole thing get going? Did the universe simply always exist? Was there a time when there was nothing?

If there was a time of nothingness, then how did the first something come into existence without a larger something to get it all started? Could there be a place for God in that process? Could he even be a *necessary* piece of the mystery of the origins of the universe?"

3. What is it about the McLaren books that gives the author hope? Does the message seem hopeful to you? Why (not)?

4. We often think of Calvin as a reformer because of specific reforms he introduced to the church. Is there a difference between signing on to Reformed beliefs as accepted dogma and having a reformational attitude or spirit? What aspects of the church are in need of reform today?

5. What happened to the author on the hill that morning? Have you had a similar experience? How would you describe it?

6. Why does the author want to jump back into the Text after the hill-top experience? What do you think she was looking for? Have you ever felt a sudden urge to read the Bible? Did you find what were you looking for? How?

7. Despite having read sympathetic writers, the author still expresses some trepidation about sharing her thoughts with another person. What does that tell us about the power and importance of personal interaction, genuine friendship, and an understanding community? What characteristics do we look for in those with whom we chose to share our journeys? What can we do to develop those characteristics ourselves?

8. Is it a coincidence that the first two people the author chose to share her journey with had been on a similar journey? Are there many people in your church who have similar doubts but are afraid to express them? Do people who have doubts and questions make better listeners? Do you have friends or family with whom you discuss your questions and doubts?

9. A few studies have shown that one of the main reasons young people leave the church is because they are discouraged from expressing doubts and asking fundamental questions. Is the attempt to get them to accept a pre-packaged theology the very thing that is causing them to reject it? What's a better approach? What should we do

if we're forced to choose between accepting people with doubts and preserving a theological tradition?

10. I might believe that some Japanese sentence is true because my Japanese friend tells me it is, even if I don't understand Japanese myself. Do we find ourselves in a similar position with respect to some of our church's doctrines? Is there a difference between believing that something is true on the basis of a (perhaps trusted) authority and believing something because you understand and have thought about it yourself? What are the advantages and disadvantages of each?

11. What can we learn from the author's observations about transplanting flowers? What are our roots? What can we do to plant them more firmly?

12. What's your impression of a church known as "the church people can come to if they don't have everything figured out, where it's okay to have more questions than answers"? Did you know people are looking for such churches? Does your home church have that reputation? Why (not)?

Chapter 13

1. Have strangers who didn't "fit in" entered your life or church community unexpectedly? Did that encounter have an impact on them? On you?

2. Have you ever been the object of kindness or generosity from an unexpected source? What was (or could be) learned from such an experience?

3. Did you find it surprising that a Muslim woman would be so gracious to Americans, in light of America's recent wars and hostilities in Muslim countries and our unjust treatment of US Muslims? Would you react the same way if a group of unknown Muslims unexpectedly came walking through your neighborhood?

4. What experiences have you had with people of other religions? What did you learn from them? Would you be willing to seek out such an experience?

5. In what way does the author "let go of God"? Is that something you resonate with? Does it seem scary?

6. What do you think the author means by "While theology and doctrine can be helpful tools when kept in proper perspective, they are not the substance of true faith"? What is the true substance of faith?

7. Are we pictures of God to the world? What do others actually learn about God by watching us?

8. What two cross-related things is the author is trying to reconcile? What does it mean to "take up your cross"? How should we do that?

9. How successful are we as individuals, as a community, or as a country at "loving our enemies"? What could we do to better love our enemies?

10. What did the author's experience with Muslim hospitality teach her about evangelism? Can we apply this to our own neighborhoods? How can our churches' evangelism programs learn from this?

Chapter 14

1. What are some of the things you love about your denomination? What are some things you wish you could change?

2. What are some of the advantages and disadvantages of teaching theological doctrines to young people?

3. Have you ever left your home and come back feeling like a stranger? What can we learn from that about ourselves, our home communities, and other people and places?

4. What's your reaction to the Jewish rabbi's explanation of why some don't accept Jesus as the Messiah?

5. What does the author mean by 'Theology is the warm-up exercise, ethics is the real event'? What implications might this have for our view of people of other denominations, religions, or people of no religion?

6. What can we learn from Matthew 3:10 and Matthew 25 about the relative importance of theology in our lives?

7. The author asks why the Bible isn't just a theology text if theology is

so important? What might considering that question teach us about the Bible? About theology texts?

8. What was the difference between what the author learned about pregnancy via books and what she experienced first hand? How does that difference relate to our approaches to God?

9. What's the proper balance between orthodoxy and orthopraxy?

10. Does each denomination's set of theological doctrine have a distinct purpose in the greater body of the Christian Church? What should our attitude be toward different denominations and their different beliefs if one is a hand, one a foot, one a mouth, etc.? Are we better working together than quibbling about theology? If so, how can we work toward that goal?

Chapter 15

1. Make a list of new questions you have and discuss them with a friend or your study group.

2. Ask a stranger what questions he or she has about God or religion or life. Try to avoid answering them. Just listen.

Recommended Reading

Bell, Rob. *Velvet Elvis*. Grand Rapids: Zondervan, 2006.

——. with Don Golden. *Jesus Wants to Save Christians*. Grand Rapids: Zondervan, 2008.

Berghoef, Bryan. *Pub Theology: Beer, Conversation, and God*. Eugene: Cascade Books, 2012.

Caputo, John D. *What Would Jesus Deconstruct?* Grand Rapids: Baker Academic, 2007.

Carroll, James. *Constantine's Sword*. Boston: *Mariner Books*, 2001.

Claiborne, Shane, *The Irresistible Revolution*. Grand Rapids: Zondervan, 2006.

——. with Chris Haw, *Jesus for President*. Grand Rapids: Zondervan, 2008.

McLaren, Brian. *A Generous Orthodoxy*. Grand Rapids: Zondervan, 2004.

Rollins, Peter. *The Orthodox Heretic*. Brewster: Paraclete Press, 2009.

Suk, John. *Not Sure: A Pastor's Journey from Faith to Doubt*. Grand Rapids: Eerdmans, 2011.

Tickle, Phyllis. *The Great Emergence: How Christianity is Changing and Why*. Grand Rapids: Baker Books, 2008.

Tolstoy, Leo. *The Kingdom of God is Within You*. New York: Barnes & Noble, 2005.

Bibliography

Caputo, John D. *What Would Jesus Deconstruct?* Grand Rapids: Baker Academic, 2007.

Carroll, James. *Constantine's Sword*. Boston: *Mariner Books*, 2001

McLaren, Brian. *A Generous Orthodoxy*. Grand Rapids: Zondervan, 2004.

Tolstoy, Leo. *The Kingdom of God is Within You*. New York: Barnes & Noble, 2005.